Nurturing Children through Preschool and Reception

The preschool and reception years can be viewed as a stage of preparation for formal schooling. But we must not lose sight of the profound impact this time of play and exploration has as children continue developing the core processes they will later rely on. *Nurturing Children through Preschool and Reception* explores how a child's mind and body develops during this critical and sensitive period and how the choices practitioners and parents make every day have a deep impact on these processes. Underpinned by the latest research in the fields of child development, psychology, health and well-being, it explores the practices that can be embedded straight away to support children's ongoing development and give them the best opportunities for future success.

The book follows a holistic approach through the Nurturing Childhoods Pedagogical Framework and the ABCs of Developing Engagement, alongside methods to consider the impact of learning experiences, decoding children's evolving behaviours and strategies for their development. Chapters cover:

- Managing the expectations placed on the early years

- Connecting with children through communication, movement and play

- Recognising emotions and promoting effective choices

- Helping young children manage their emotions in a social world

- Developing young children's confidence to think and express themselves

- Understanding young children's friendships and conflicts

- Supporting lifelong learning in the years before school

Part of the *Nurturing Childhoods* series, this exciting book provides practitioners and parents with the knowledge and understanding they need to nurture children's happiness, well-being and sense of security through the preschool and reception years.

Kathryn Peckham is a childhood consultant, researcher, author and founder of Nurturing Childhoods. She is an active member of global Early Childhood networks, conducting research for governments and international organisations, writing curricula and contributing to industry-leading publications and guidance such as Birth to 5 Matters.

Nurturing Children through Preschool and Reception

Developing the Potential of Every Child

Kathryn Peckham

Routledge
Taylor & Francis Group

LONDON AND NEW YORK

Designed cover image: © Getty Images

First published 2024
by Routledge
4 Park Square, Milton Park, Abingdon, Oxon, OX14 4RN

and by Routledge
605 Third Avenue, New York, NY 10158

Routledge is an imprint of the Taylor & Francis Group, an informa business

© 2024 Kathryn Peckham

British Library Cataloguing-in-Publication Data
A catalogue record for this book is available from the British Library

ISBN: 978-1-032-35472-9 (hbk)
ISBN: 978-1-032-35471-2 (pbk)
ISBN: 978-1-003-32704-2 (ebk)

DOI: 10.4324/9781003327042

Typeset in Bembo
by SPi Technologies India Pvt Ltd (Straive)

Contents

Acknowledgements

It is with such great pleasure that I am able to share this series of books with you all. They have been many years in the creating and with numerous people to thank. Firstly, the staff and children at Olney Preschool and Olney Infant Academy in Buckingham-shire, England, the settings of the original research where I shared two years with the most delightful children and wonderfully accommodating and passionate staff.

I would also like to acknowledge the support of Bright Horizons Family Solutions UK, in providing images to illustrate the practice promoted in these publications. The Creative Services team at Bright Horizons worked collaboratively with me to supply the many delightful images of children and their carers engaging in playful and sensitive interactions. The images in these books were captured in various Bright Horizons nurseries throughout England and Scotland and with the kind permission of the parents to use these images of their fabulous children.

And I would like to thank my colleagues and friends at the Centre for Research in Early Childhood in Birmingham, most notably Professor Chris Pascal and Professor Tony Bertram who listened tirelessly to my thoughts and ideas, helping me to unravel my excited sparks of inspiration into well considered observations. A colleague once said to me that true creativity comes from the combination of knowledge, skill, inspiration and persistence all of which were nurtured by this dynamic duo.

But as always, none of this would be possible without the ongoing love and support of my amazing husband and children who never stop believing in me. You have been there to read, to listen and on occasion to add some unique perspectives, all the while keeping me laughing… and fed! I could not do this without you.

Section I
Introduction

Nurturing childhoods for all our tomorrows

Whether you are caring for your first child, running a chain of busy preschools or responsible for a school district, you will have your own reasons for reading these books. But the fact that you are would suggest that you are well aware of the tremendous impact we all have on the children in our lives through every decision we make, through every experience we facilitate and every interaction we share. In previous books in this series we have looked at what this means as we nurture preverbal, pre-mobile children, dependent on us for many of their experiences. We have looked at nurturing the expanding world of a toddler as they get to their feet, exploring, interacting and developing a growing sense of all that they are. Now, in this book we will focus our attentions on slightly older children, with a few years of experiences influencing the ways in which they engage with their world.

When we start talking about nurturing young children, it can seem like everyone has an opinion. You may have experienced this for yourself with advice, good and bad, coming at you from every direction. After all, we were all a child once, we have all had a childhood and experiences of what that meant to us. And we all have a vested interest in nurturing our children's futures, whether we are parents or not. However, books written on the growth and development of children, both in their early years and in the school classroom, can typically centre around the curriculums governing them and the learning goals and objectives that children are intended to work towards. There are a number of concerns with this top-down approach that can change in line with some new directive at any moment. Our children are too important to not look beyond a "one size fits all" curriculum, programme or approach and after decades of practice, research and frustrations the time has come to offer a different way.

The books in the Nurturing Childhoods series will help you to look at the whole child, not as machines that produce the desired outcome provided we invest in the right

DOI: 10.4324/9781003327042-1

programmes, but as children. We will look at the foundations of learning and development, yes, but we will also look at what it means to nurture a child mindful of the many influences on their lives; responding to the many environments they are in, the interactions they experience and their vulnerability to every emotion surrounding them. They are a product of every experience they have ever had and deeply impacted by the decisions being made on their behalf.

It is only when we recognise this that we can show our children the possibilities that exist in the world and nurture the dispositions they need to go out and grasp them. If we don't, the unique potential residing in every child can become devalued, derailed and ultimately we all lose out as they simply disengage – something you may have already experienced yourself as a child. So, join me as we start looking beyond our adult agendas and look instead at the children in front of us as together we develop the potential of all our children.

Navigating your way around the series

There are four books in the series: *Nurturing Babies, Nurturing Toddlers; Nurturing Children through Preschool and Reception* and *Nurturing Through the Primary Years* (Figure S1.1). Whilst these may sound similar to labels you may be familiar with through childcare and school establishments, each with its age boundaries and transitions, look again. There are no age-related boundaries here. Whilst the way you care for and engage with a child will develop and mature, this must be in response to the child in front of you, rather than any arbitrary calendar dates. Otherwise you can become focused on where a child "should be", whilst losing sight of the development that is occurring right now, areas that need revisiting or those in which they are racing ahead.

In the first book in this series we focused our attentions on the needs and developments of preverbal children not yet able to freely navigate the world around them. Then, in *Nurturing Toddlers*, we drew our attention to children who are getting to their feet and exploring more independently. In this book we will look at children with a few more years' worth of experiences influencing all they do. And then in the final book of this series, we will turn our attentions to exploring the different realities faced by children as they enter more formal environments of learning.

The books also celebrate the fact that children are on a lifelong journey of holistic, interconnected and continuously evolving development. Because of this, many of the themes running through the books are relevant for all children and the intention is that you enjoy them all. For example, I have a chapter in this book called "Supporting Young Children's Developing Behaviours", now that their years of experience in a range of environments are seeing their learnt behaviours beginning to embed. That does not mean that their experiences of emotions, behaviours and the responses they have received to them have not been deeply informative already; they will continue to

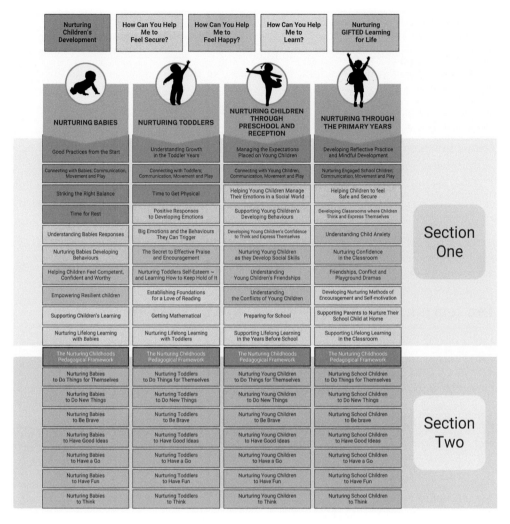

Figure S1.1 The four books in this series, exploring the growth and development of children throughout their early childhood and on into the school classroom.

be so as their automatic responses are honed. And we will touch on the emotional needs of all children throughout the chapter. A child's need for effective communication, expanding language and sustained play continue to be core themes, especially as transitions to more formal learning environments are being considered.

Through these books I want you to learn something, but I won't achieve this by simply telling you what I think and expecting you to do the same. Instead, I offer you the child development, biological or psychological theory relevant to the chapter, unpick and demonstrate the relevance this has and then offer you suggestions as you develop your own confident and consistent practice. With every chapter written using the Nurturing Childhoods approach of Knowledge, Understanding and then Support, you will then have all you need to develop practices that are right for you and the children in your life.

Each section is intended to help you think and reflect, but through their accessible style of writing and illustrations, they can be easily and quickly understood without the need for previous knowledge and are intended to be read and understood by anyone with an interest in young children. And because of their foundation in child development (rather than any curriculum, programme or approach), they will always remain relevant, regardless of changes in educational policy or documentation. This is also true wherever in the world you live, the programmes or policies that govern you, even the decade in which you read these words because nurturing practice and understanding is both timeless and universal.

They are also further supported by a setting-based accreditation and a suite of online courses for parents, practitioners and teachers. You can even join the Nurturing Childhoods Community, share your experiences and receive tons of support and guidance, so for more information head to, free workbooks and supplemental materials, head to nurturingchildhoods.com.

The learning child... yes – but what about the rest?

As you will know if you have any children in your life, they are all very much their own person. Whilst they are learning continuously, through every experience, they are deeply impacted by the realities central to their lives. Experiences will depend on where the children live and the people and resources that surround them, as well as the attitudes and responses that become familiar. How – and what – a child learns through an experience will also be influenced by their own responses, which are developing through every previous experience they have had. Trying to cater for every child's needs as if they are the same is then not only unhelpful, but it also does our children a gross misservice. However, when an approach is centred around a governing curriculum, learning goals and objectives, it provides a structure that children are then intended to fit around, essentially focusing on one aspect of the multitude of factors influencing a growing, developing child.

While it is really important to keep a watchful eye on a child's development, alert to any concerns that may need some extra support, a child is more than a product of their development goals. These books think of children and how we nurture the full scope of their learning and development in a very different way. And it does this by bringing our focus back to the child, recognising that development is complex, diverse and dependent on many factors and cannot possibly be nurtured until we have explored the wider implications of what it means to be THIS child in THIS moment, who will be greatly influenced by the world around them.

Throughout my years of managing nurseries and advising schools, settings and families, I have seen some amazing things. But where practice has been limited, this has tended to be from a lack of understanding of what a child needs, the realities of being them in this moment, influenced by every experience that has gone before and the impact we are having. But this requires us to stop for a moment and question the way things have been done in the past, to reflect on what we are doing now and to ask ourselves why – especially now when focus can become trained on very young children's readiness for formal education and processes of learning that they are not yet ready for.

As a species, we are hardwired to be curious and increasingly independent, social, self-motivated and courageous. These character traits, and others besides, have enabled us to learn and thrive for hundreds of thousands of years, capable of levels of collaboration needed to establish complex societies, employing intuition that allows us to know what others may be thinking and using these skills to work towards complex shared goals. Our young children have been discovering and developing these powerful tools of learning from the moment they were born. As we now focus on children with a few more years experiences behind them, we will see the impact of all of these, and the responses a child has received, taking root and informing the chance that they will do so again. Acting as gatekeepers to their experiences, we play a tremendous role through every decision, environment and permission we extend. And with every experience informing the next, we are also deeply influencing a child's ongoing disposition towards these characteristics. Will they develop along positive trajectories as our children become more confident, motivated and curious in the world around them? Or will their experiences see them become more timid and reluctant to engage? How do the experiences we offer stimulate our children? Or are they learning that this might not be worth their efforts? Do they receive encouragement when they want to go outside and explore or are they dissuaded through our environments, responses or routines?

When we can set aside the blinkers of curriculum expectations and look instead with these deep-rooted processes in mind, we can learn so much more about the journey a child is on than any curriculum guide can begin to tell us. And we can know so much more about where this journey is likely to take them. But we need to know what to look for and to understand the difference we make every day to the process. We have then been exploring these tools or developing "characteristics" of lifelong learning and the dispositions children develop towards using them throughout this series. In *Nurturing Babies* and *Nurturing Toddlers*, I introduced you to GIFTED Learning (the Greater Involvement Facilitated Through Engaging in Dispositions) and is something we will revisit again in Chapter 10.

We will take a look at the holistic nature of a child, rooted in their need for engagement, movement and play. We will look at what it means for a child to feel secure, understanding how their behaviours reflect their well-being and engagement. And we will look at how our environments, interactions and every decision we make feeds into a child's growing sense of agency and the factors that go a long way to determining their happiness. And as we begin to look towards the more formal environments of learning that they will soon be transitioning to, recognise that the confidence, curiosity and love of enquiry they enter with will be far more important than the numbers or letters they know already. And just how much their growing independence, social skills and ability to engage will influence the ease of this transition, how well they respond and settle into their new environment and the ongoing success they will experience within it.

We know the importance of a child's well-being and involvement from the work of many esteemed colleagues in the field of early years. You may also be familiar with the idea of there being a hierarchy of needs that need addressing. And yet, if we find ourselves overly concerned with development goals, we can lose sight of this and the impact that we ourselves are having. Meaningful learning simply isn't possible if a child does not feel safe and secure in their surroundings. And unless we learn to see children in a more holistic way, the whole set-up is prone to topple. However, many childcare and teaching qualifications can lack focus in these areas.

In Section 1 you will then find chapters looking at how we nurture young children's development, how we help children to feel secure, how we can help them find their happiness and then how we can nurture a growing love of learning and enquiry, all while offering the experiences so important to learning and the development of dispositions common to enthusiastic, lifelong learners (Figure S1.2).

In Section 2 I will then continue to explore the Nurturing Childhoods Pedagogical Framework (NCPF) first introduced in *Nurturing Babies* and then extended in *Nurturing Toddlers* as we explore a new way of thinking about children's development and the way you observe and facilitate it. Through the NCPF, aka The Flower, we recognise that children's processes of growth and development have remained fundamentally unchanged for hundreds of thousands of years. Whether you are working in the UK, the USA or the UAE; whether you follow a Montessori, High Scope or Forest School Approach; whether you care for children in a huge centre, a forest or your spare room, or as parents, practitioners, teachers or family support workers. By recognising core characteristics that are developing in all our children, recognising the behaviours that demonstrate them and keeping our CHILDREN at the centre of all we do, we learn to stop tying ourselves up in knots over external agendas that can change at any moment.

But to do this we must embrace a child's holistic, continual and constantly evolving development, recognising that it is embedded within the environments we give them access to, the interactions we share and the permissions we offer them to engage. The success of these processes is reflected in the behaviours and responses being demonstrated, but to see them our focus needs to be on the child in front of us, mindful that they are more than a demonstration of their learning goals. When we can do that, children flourish in the ways they have been instinctively trying to do for millennia. They can do so as babies, toddlers… and all the way through the school system. In ways that protect them from changing directives, unknown futures and the realities of a universally connected world.

As I have said in previous books, while this at first may seem a little more complex than a development framework you are familiar with, child development is complex. Children are multifaceted, changing minute by minute and vulnerable to any number of influences. They will not demonstrate all they are through an activity designed last

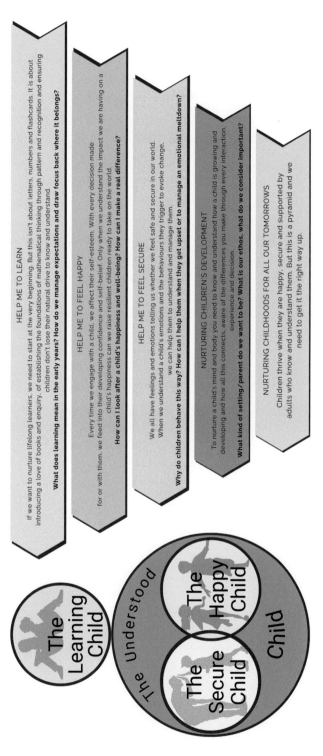

Nurturing The Whole Child:
Happy, Secure and Ready to Take on the World

HELP ME TO LEARN

If we want to nurture lifelong learners, we need to start at the very beginning. But this isn't about letters, numbers and flashcards. It is about introducing a love of books and enquiry, of establishing the foundations of mathematical thinking through pattern and recognition and ensuring children don't lose their natural drive to know and understand.

What does learning mean in the early years? How do we manage expectations and draw focus back where it belongs?

HELP ME TO FEEL HAPPY

Every time we engage with a child, we affect their self-esteem. With every decision made for or with them, we feed into their developing confidence and self-belief. Only when we understand the impact we are having on a child's happiness can we raise resilient children ready to take on the world.

How can I look after a child's happiness and well-being? How can I make a real difference?

HELP ME TO FEEL SECURE

We all have feelings and emotions telling us whether we feel safe and secure in our world. When we understand a child's emotions and the behaviours they trigger to evoke change, we can help them to understand and manage them.

Why do children behave this way? How can I help them when they get upset or to manage an emotional meltdown?

NURTURING CHILDREN'S DEVELOPMENT

To nurture a child's mind and body you need to know and understand how a child is growing and developing and how all this connects, aware of the differences you make through every interaction, experience and decision.

What kind of setting/parent do we want to be? What is our ethos, what do we consider important?

NURTURING CHILDHOODS FOR ALL OUR TOMORROWS

Children thrive when they are happy, secure and supported by adults who know and understand them. But this is a pyramid and we need to get it the right way up.

The Learning Child

The Understood Child

The Happy Child

The Secure Child

Figure S1.2 Developing the learning skills and capabilities of a child might be at the top of our agenda, but it rests on so much more that we need to get right first.

week to meet today's learning goals. But they do speak volumes through every behaviour and response, provided you know how to see them. If you want to capture this level of understanding of the children in your life, not only do you need to be led by the child in front of you, but you also need methods that will allow for deeper reflection and a more informed awareness of the experiences you offer. By the time you have finished reading this series, you will then have all of that too.

Navigating your way around this book

In Section 1 of this book we will be taking a look at the effects of different experiences on young children, especially on the lead-up to school classrooms and how their changing abilities and interests need to be nurtured, explored and be given the room to be set free. We will continue to look at the importance of communication, movement and play in the minds and bodies of young children as we explore their tremendous potential. And we will look at how opportunities for rich, meaningful play will have far greater long-term potential than the achievement of any short-term goals.

As we explore helping young children to feel secure, we will look at their developing emotions now they find themselves managing more complex social situations and needing to recognise emotions in others. We will consider the expectations placed on young children and what happens when ineffectual techniques are used. We will investigate what is driving children's natural behavioural instincts as we help them to recognise these and promote effective choices as we give them increasing ownership. And we will look at what it means when we promote a young child's abilities to think for themselves, to express an opinion and find their voice and the impact this will have on them in the years to come.

As we look at helping young children to feel happy, we will explore the social skills children are developing, the play opportunities that are becoming increasingly important and the measures that can be put in place when children are struggling. We will examine how children make friendships in the early years, how these friendships are maturing and how you can support children as they learn to respond to social challenges and conflict.

And as we look at helping young children to learn, we will explore the abilities they are developing that will help them manage in the school classroom, the rich experiences that are providing essential foundations and the consequences when these are misplaced. We will look at what it means to continue nurturing engaged, motivated learners, mindful of how children's approaches to learning are maturing and the deeply influential opportunities and resources children need during this time to embed dispositions of lifelong learning in the years before school.

As I have said throughout the books in this series, children need to feel happy and secure before they can settle into any higher-order activities. They are developing in response to all the opportunities that surround them. And they have minds and bodies

Chapters exploring the importance of nurturing children's holistic development

NURTURING CHILDREN IN THE EARLY YEARS

As we explore how children's minds and bodies are growing in the early years we will consider the magnitude of impact and the differences you make every time you talk to a baby, listen to a toddler or engage in a hunt for spiders with older children. We will look at the expectations placed on children and those caring for them and refocus our attention where it is really important. We will look at what happens when you play with a child, making eye contact and engaging, as well as provide lots of practical advice and guidance.

HOW CAN YOU HELP ME TO FEEL SECURE?

These chapters will help you look at children's developing emotions and behaviours. We consider how we can help children to understand their emotions, how we can support them to express themselves and make friends and, as the child matures, how to manage more difficult behaviours, supporting children to feel safe and secure, able to express themselves and make friends, even when experiencing the tough emotions that we can all experience.

HOW CAN YOU HELP ME TO FEEL HAPPY?

Whilst we can't make a child feel happy, or feel any emotion for that matter, we can help them to develop their confidence, their self-esteem and resilience. We can support them as they find their place in this social world, able to make friends, express their needs and feel capable of achieving that which would make them happy, all with a growth mindset that sees them take life's setbacks with an air of optimism rather than defeat.

HOW CAN YOU HELP ME TO LEARN?

These chapters look at supporting our children's learning from day one. But rather than letters, numbers and flashcards and a programme of activities, we look instead at the practices we can introduce to support a love of books and enquiry, of establishing the foundations of mathematical thinking through pattern, observation and purpose and ensuring children don't lose the natural drive to know and understand that they are born with. All of this begins from the tiniest babies and continues into the primary years.

NURTURING GIFTED LEARNING FOR LIFE

In Section 2 we will explore the Nurturing Childhoods Pedagogical Framework (NCPF) as a new way to understand and nurture a GIFTED Learning approach. Keeping children very much at the centre of all we do, the NCPF recognises the Greater Involvement we can Facilitate when children Engage in their Dispositions as we will explore this through seven critical behaviours in line with the growing capabilities of the child in focus. It will look at why this is so important, their impact on future attitudes towards learning and how this can all be nurtured from day one.

Figure S1.3 Through these chapters we will explore the importance of nurturing children holistically throughout their early childhood and the primary years.

growing through the same mechanisms and processes that have ensured our survival as a species for hundreds of thousands of years. But to nurture this in our children means placing THEM at the centre of all we do. In Section 2 we will then look again at the Nurturing Childhoods Pedagogical Framework (NCPF) that does just that. The NCPF was first introduced in *Nurturing Babies* and developed in *Nurturing Toddlers* with the ABCs of Developing Engagement (ABCoDE). Now, as we consider children with a few more years of learning experiences behind them, I will add a method that will allow you to look at the impact these experiences are having on your children. Through the OPTED Scale, we will take our next step towards nurturing childhoods.

In the final chapters, we will look at all our young children are communicating to us through their evolving behaviours and the powerful ways we have to nurture their development through some key practices. With the help of the NCPF, the ABCoDE and the OPTED Scale, we can then re-evaluate the choices we extend to our children and the opportunities these choices offer for them to think, to try, to do and have fun.

Igniting the potential of dispositional development

You do not need to spend long talking with a young child, watching them play or observing their interactions to know that all these processes are deeply rooted in any number of influences. Their responses in the sandpit may be very different to those observed when they were choosing a book; this will also significantly depend on whether they were on their own or the selection of friends that were with them… even if it were a Monday or a Friday. All of this illustrates just how dynamic and fluid the processes of learning and development are, with almost limitless variables impacting every child and influencing every moment you share. And yet in a landscape where recognised progress will often hinge on the abilities a child can demonstrate within predefined developmental milestones, many foundational experiences can be over-looked, along with many of the realities facing our children as the powerful dispositions they are born with are devalued.

Imagine if we did not focus on development goals and were instead able to accom-pany predetermined metrics with methods and techniques that could capture the indi-vidual responses of a child in the moment. Think what could be possible if every child's natural instincts for knowing and understanding the world and its people were recog-nised and developed throughout their childhood. What could be possible if the moti-vation and curiosity you see in a young child exploring something that interests them were maintained? What might they learn if their desires to know "How?", "Who?", "What?", "Where?" were encouraged? What might they be driven to do if their curi-osity and growing independence never left them? But to keep these instincts through-out their childhood, children need ongoing experiences that cultivate their courage, persistence and a belief in their own potential for success. They need exciting opportu-nities that take their imagination and curiosity to the next level, whilst experiencing the power that comes from seeing what they can achieve. This all speaks of dispositional development.

Whilst a child's opportunities will inevitably be largely guided by adults throughout their day, if the richness of these experiences is limited to demonstrating external agendas, developmental objectives or acquired skills, we significantly restrain their potential for growth in ways that reverberate throughout their emotional and social well-being. We must then look to understand and preserve these innate behaviours in our children, encouraging their natural curiosity and inclinations whilst showing them the potential that exists all around them. This involves allowing children a voice; it means granting them agency and opportunities for independent thought, supported by advocates who champion their right to ponder, to question and to imagine as they demonstrate their full range of capabilities, not just to an onlooker, but to themselves.

The methods you will gain through reading the Nurturing Childhoods series are all underpinned by a longitudinal phenomenological study and decades of research (Peckham, 2021), providing you with a comprehensive and holistic framework for understanding your children's development. These insights can be seamlessly integrated with any curriculum, program or approach, allowing you to consider the impact of your actions and interactions and your environments and pedagogies, both formal and informal. This empowers you to not only capture the intricate constructs inherent in learning and development, but also the social and cultural dynamics that shape children's experiences and the ultimate outcomes they will attain. It recognises the profound influence that pedagogical choices wield on a child's depth of engagement and their evolving attitudes towards learning, both in the moment and as their predispositions take root. So, as you embark on the journey of nurturing your children during their early years, I hope this book encourages you to re-evaluate the experiences you are offering, mindful of their deeper potential as you tap into these fundamental human instincts that have propelled us all towards staggering levels of learning from our first days of life.

Reference

Peckham, K. (2021) A phenomenological study exploring how early childhood pedagogies enable the development of dispositions. Doctoral thesis, Birmingham City University.

Managing the expectations placed on young children

We all have experience of being parented and educated during our childhood. No matter by whom or the style that was used, for better or worse we all have that experience informing the ways we now care for and respond to children. Whether your intentions are to give the children in your life the exact same experiences you once had or whether you intend to do things completely different, you have probably heard familiar phrases coming out of your own mouth and perhaps even those of the children.

When you think or read about "how" you might offer a nurturing approach to support children's learning, you may come across the term pedagogy. If you have already read the first two books in this series, you will even be familiar with the Nurturing Childhoods Pedagogical Framework. A pedagogy is then a way of thinking about the set of techniques and strategies that you use to support the learning taking place – encouraging children to master new abilities, to develop new skills and gain more knowledge as they experience their learning. Far from a label you assign yourself, your pedagogy should be a fluid process between you and the child in front of you as you provide opportunities for them to develop their skills and learning dispositions and as they gain knowledge and an interest in the process of learning, all within the particular environment and social groupings you find yourself in.

But nurturing children is not as simple as considering a set of techniques you might consider to be beneficial. You must also consider how children learn and progress. How their young bodies are growing daily, how their responses are affected by their social skills and emotional stability, their state of mind and, let's face it, what they had for breakfast! Reminiscent of Maslow and his hierarchy of needs, any action or behaviour you are trying to encourage within a child will be motivated by certain physiological needs. Only when feeling secure, with all of their basic needs met, can a child turn their attention to being all they can be. You may have experienced this for yourself when starting a new position. With no secure attachments or friends around you, you will remember feeling the need to make connections before thoughts can turn to the great

DOI: 10.4324/9781003327042-2

work you might do there. And you certainly would not have been in the mood for much conversation if you were feeling in need of a bathroom. So, as you read through these books, I remind you to keep this holistic view.

Knowledge

Know what to consider when thinking about nurturing children in the years before school

Before we consider any external expectations placed on children we must then place the child and their needs at the centre of all we do. This might sound obvious and without debate, but read that sentence again…. Do you really? … Everything?

Every moment of a child's early life is precious and should be valued for the possibilities it offers. So, what does this tell us about how we should nurture children and the approaches we need to consider? Essentially it focuses our attention on the fact that we are talking about children with complex feelings and needs – not simply the source of another completed list of ticked goals. Before we can realise any aspirations of a child achieving their full potential, we need to consider their comfort levels within the environment, their sense of safety and security, the attachments they are making and the relationships that are forming. While attachments are often highly considered with very young children, they can become overlooked as a child gets older,

Figure 1.1 First and foremost, children need to feel happy and secure in their environment. This comes from being surrounded by adults they know and trust with lots of memories of having their needs met.

yet this is highly relevant to us all, no matter our age or situation (Figure 1.1).

If you want children to be open to possibility, to push themselves and what they are capable of, they need to be given the space and permission to do so. They need to feel that they can come to you when they need you for support – but after they have had a chance to grapple with ideas themselves. They need to experience what it means to make their own choices and to trial their own ideas, even when this results in failure. They also need to experience making decisions for themselves and to not feel guilty when doing something that others may feel differently about. But to do all of this requires an environment where children can experience a level of autonomy, where they can experience what it means to be them.

Children growing and learning in a highly governed environment of expected behaviours miss out on these opportunities to pursue answers to their own questions or to challenge the limits of what is expected. It is then so important that we recognise the impact we are having, both directly and indirectly, through the environments, activities and messages we offer. Observe carefully as they spend time with you. How are their bodies and minds engaged? What learning is occurring in this moment? What memories are being made? And what opportunities do your children have to impact all the above? Take this time to marvel in all the tremendous growth that is occurring throughout their systems, knowing that the impact of these moments will stay with them for the rest of their lives.

Developing a consistent approach

When you think about caring for a child and the methods and practices you want to employ today, you may have various things to think about. What community do you live in, what are the child's previous experiences and their home environment like? What opportunities can you offer, inside and out? What are their current interests, capabilities and developing skills? What have they done before? What are they on the verge of doing now? While you may have a curriculum, structure or guide that you need to consider, if you want your approach to be carried out with consistency and confidence you may also like to think about a style of approach. Of course you may have a style determined for you. Whether this is play-based, inquiry-based, project-based or more of a direct teaching approach, it is vital that you keep the individual child, the circumstance and even the weather firmly in mind as you take advantage of the opportunities that come your way.

Routine and structure or child-led learning

One of the biggest changes children experience during their early educational transitions is that from an environment focused on child-led learning to one more focused on routines and structure. So, should we be introducing this in the lead-up to the school classroom? Children do need a level of structure and rules in order to feel safe and secure. And as a trusted adult within their young life, you are going to need some of these rules, together with a structure behind them that is carefully thought through and established. But children also need to feel like a valued member of the group, they need to feel engaged in their environment and a very real part of its construction.

Children learn best in the here and now, in situations that are important to them, as they develop skills "Just in time. Not just in case!" When you plan their activities weeks in advance or expect them to adhere to overly structured timetables throughout the day, you are missing out on their natural desire to enquire and investigate what pops into their head. When you stop their explorations prematurely because the clock suggests it is time for something else, you may be interrupting them on the verge of a great achievement, preventing them from making the next connection in their learning, understanding the next piece of the puzzle or from solving the problem they have been grappling with for some time. And whilst everything tends to stop for lunch, for all the other structured breaks in your day stop a moment and consider how necessary they are.

When you begin thinking about the rules and structure that you want to employ or you begin considering those that are already in place, start with the boundaries and structures that you feel you need to offer safety (Figure 1.2). Then consider those that allow the setting or household to function effectively. Once you have devised these two lists, consider whether the rules you already have in place are always being followed. If not, you may wish to consider a few things.

- Are the rules needed?

- Are they explicit and clear or unspoken and expected?

- Have the children been involved in devising them?

- Are they fair to everyone?

If the answer to any of these questions is no, that might explain any problems that you are experiencing. Then look at the routines and structures you have around you and ask where they have come from. Are they necessary? Are they there to support the children or to suit the adults? When we look to impose rigid routines and structure with children, especially young children, we undermine this unique period of growth and development. When we take them away from their natural methods of learning and inquiry too often, they learn not to bother. So, to make the experience of learning a success, with positive impact a child can grow and develop through, avoid becoming overly planned out and structured. Instead, immerse yourselves in the potential opportunities all around you as you share in this wonderful time together.

Figure 1.2 Rules are needed in every society, but they should be there to keep you safe, not to exert control.

Understanding

Understand the effects various approaches have on the children experiencing them

The style of care children experience has a great deal of influence on the way in which they develop. Children raised in rich environments full of opportunities to engage and play gain an understanding of themselves and the world around them. With the physical freedom to access their environment, they learn what their bodies can do and develop the skills to do more. When they have opportunities to follow their own interests they can gain instant response to their questions: what happens if, I wonder why that, who could be there? This develops their curiosity and the motivation to enquire. There is much to see, hear and comprehend and with time and space, along with the understanding and support of the adults around them, this foundational period of learning can be embraced.

Repeatedly telling a child what they should be doing or instructing their every movement, however, does not give them the opportunity to see their potential for themselves. A great deal of a child's learning comes from experiencing their mistakes, from using ineffective materials in construction or trialling inadequate tools to achieve a required result. Through their trial and improvement they are learning about cause and effect and the properties of materials as new ideas occur to them. And through this process they are gaining a view of themselves as a learner, influencing how they think of themselves and the courage they will approach the next opportunity with.

How learning styles feel to the child experiencing them

When we are learning any new skill, ability or newfound knowledge, there will be things that we need to be told. There will be some skills and techniques that you want to share with your children and areas they need instruction in. However, expecting children to think in exactly the same way you do is a dangerous place to be. The world is constantly changing and progressing and children need to develop the skills to adapt along with it. Do you really think in exactly the same way your parents did – or your grandparents? Would you want to?

When children's activities are continuously governed through a carefully managed day, their learning behaviours are essentially being controlled. As an adult in a hierarchical position of power, you are then expecting children to perform as you want at this moment in time. In some instances, this is of course a necessary part of living within a social society where there are rules to manage our safety and expectations to live by. However, continually expecting certain responses from children simply through a hierarchy of power does little to engage them in the learning process. While you might see some short-term gains, consider how your children are learning to think for themselves. How are they learning to question and to seek answers to their questions?

Children do not learn best when under constant direct supervision. Nor do they experience what they are capable of. If they are consistently being taught what to think and not how to think, they are learning to be easily manipulated into what others are telling them, at the expense of what is right for them. If their ideas are being overlooked or going unheard, how are they learning to have a voice? And if they are growing up without a voice or a choice to express the little things, how do you expect them to make the right choice in the bigger moments?

When children are frequently given the opportunity to try new things, to have a go without rigid expectations, they learn what it means to pursue answers to their own questions. When they are guided through their early years with structure and guidance, they learn what it means to think for themselves and to make a decision, seeing error as a step in the learning process. And they learn what it means to face their mistakes and manage them without fear or avoidance. If instead children are not given these opportunities, they either learn to repress their natural instincts for learning or begin to express a learned helplessness. Either of which can damage their self-esteem and see them seeking affection and approval in less positive ways.

What is the sense of learning?

As a species we are born ready and willing to learn. Everything, from every stimulation of sight, sound and taste that we are surrounded by. As I have explored in previous books in this series, these natural desires to learn are necessary to make the thousand trillion connections we need to wire up our developing brain. It is what makes us so adaptable to living within the environments and situations that we inhabit all over the globe. It is why our babies are so keen to touch, explore and put everything in their mouths; why our mobile toddlers never want to sit still, seeking stimulation throughout their developing body; and why our older children are desperately keen to investigate, to make social connections and find out why (Figure 1.3).

Then they reach the age of, in some cases, four years old and are expected to sit still in a classroom. Resisting all these natural instincts to move and, instead, learn in an adult-imposed way. And we wonder why our children get fidgety and our school children "Don't like school", quickly disengaging from the learning process when they have been so in tune with it. They are compelled to engage in the multisensory learning and physical learning techniques that have been hugely powerful since birth.

Figure I.3 Powerful mechanisms of learning are driving us to want to know, explore and understand. This doesn't start at any particular age, nor does it change when we reach some other milestone. There is a reason I talk of Lifelong Learning!

We now have the neuroscience to demonstrate how impactful this is to growth and development. Studies have shown that children raised in an environment where they have been given opportunities to engage in positive, sensory-rich experiences develop brains more densely packed with the connections associated with healthy growth.

Early childhood is a critical time for this development to occur and any core experiences that have been missed during this vital time will not be easily made up for in later life. You will have experienced this if you have ever tried to learn a new language as an adult, something young children seem to pick up with ease. Or, if you have spoken to a child from a language-poor environment who is now struggling to acquire the speech patterns they are going to need for school. Or the child who was not given enough opportunities to strengthen their core muscles in the early years and is now struggling to sit up straight, slouching in chairs and quickly becoming uncomfortable.

Support

Be supported to consider what might work for you, your children and the families you work with

During this time, no toy, resource or structured approach to learning is as valuable as the moments of engagement and understanding that you are offering to a child. Every minute of these precious years should be cherished and seen for the gifts that you can offer them. That doesn't mean purchasing every item in the catalogue or feeling guilty about the tasks you need to perform. But it does mean mindfully connecting with them when you are with them and being aware of the impact your words and actions are having on them.

Turn off the distractions and have a conversation. Be mindful of the expectations you place on them. Look into their eyes and really connect, taking advantage of any opportunity when they offer this to you. And find time every day to connect with every child. Whether this is over a meal, a story or supporting the construction of a life-sized model of crocodile. When you appreciate just how engaged their young minds and bodies are and you can respect their powerful drives to explore and understand the world, it becomes more important to facilitate the opportunities they need. Allow them to meaningfully gain experiences, to investigate and to feel the result of their actions and to be mindful of the children who may not readily put themselves forward.

Planning a day of engaged learning

The best form of planning is about ensuring children have the environment, resources, stimulation and support to engage their bodies and minds as they need to. Children are developing every moment of every day. This is not something you can sit and plan for weeks in advance in anything more than a generic sense. How do you know what children are going to be interested in? All of them?

Ask yourself how the experiences you offer to children, in the time frames that you are offering them, allow for children's natural desires to learn.

- Can children access what they need when they need it, in the way they want to explore it?

- Can they mix resources and experiences?

■ Can they freely move around the environment, inside and out as they combine the opportunities in each?

■ Can they trial their ideas, think about things for a while and come back later? Perhaps tomorrow?

■ Can they experience a challenge or take a risk, building their skills and confidence with each attempt?

■ Is there opportunity and a need for working together with a friend, allowing them to respond to each other's ideas and suggestions?

Begin by considering the routine and structure that need to be in place. Possibly the start and end of the day, lunchtime or scheduled visits. For everything else, ask yourself whether that item in the planning is as important as children's explorations. Does it have to happen then? In that way? Every time? If your answer is yes, can you answer why? If your honest answer to that question stems from anything other than "because it is best for the children," perhaps think again.

Making and following rules

Firstly, take the time to talk to your children about the decisions, rules and guidelines that are being employed as you use this opportunity to actively boost their conscious behaviours. Simply telling a child "Because I said so" teaches them little about the reasoning behind what you are saying, or how they can use this to inform future decisions they may need to make when you are not around to guide them. Talking to them about the guidelines and structures you need to have in place will help them to think about what they are doing and why. This also promotes a greater degree of honesty and confidence, which will be reflected in the qualities that they grow up to embrace.

Next, invite children to suggest the rules that they think are important. Encourage open discussions about the different ideas that are put forward, why this might be important and the benefits of their suggestions being in place. When you support the children to write the rules, help them to express them positively; so "No hitting" becomes "We use gentle hands," "No running indoors" becomes "We walk inside". You can then invite the children to draw pictures, to collage or to add the embellishments that will help them to remember.

You might also like to think of a different heading, so instead of "Class Rules", perhaps "Reasons Our Class Is Great." And if these rules are forgotten, use gentle reminders and direct children's attention back to this joint task and the reasons you all did it.

Physical learning

Children's muscles, bones and internal processes are developing daily through the physical opportunities they are offered. But these need challenging, testing and developing as the limits of their abilities are explored and pushed further. The only person who can do this is the one who can feel the emotions and responses these explorations generate: the child themselves.

Now more fully aware of their own bodies, children need to experience what it can do. They also need opportunities to take risks and experience manageable challenges, pushing the limits of what they can achieve. Without these safe opportunities under your watchful eye, children will not learn how to manage risk without becoming frightened of it. When they are then faced with bigger risks, perhaps without a

Figure 1.4 With every physical act children are developing strength in their muscles and bones, along with learning how to use them. Only then will they be ready for the more demanding challenges they will meet.

more mature safety net, they may find themselves challenged in ways they are not experienced enough to manage. But, be mindful that their understanding of their capabilities may be less than realistic. Their physical development requires lots of physical opportunities to stretch, leap, spin, jump and lift together with sympathetic support and gentle encouragement when things do not initially pan out, along with lots of opportunities for exhausted little bodies to rest (Figure 1.4).

Experiential learning

As we have learnt, with every experience, children are making connections deep within their brain, forming the structures and pathways to determine all future responses. As experiential learners, children need rich and varied, hands-on experiences. And when multiple senses are involved in an experience, even more connections are being made. So think for a moment of the experiences you are offering your children and the senses that they are engaging. Imagine slicing open a juicy orange; the vibrant colours, the smell, the juice trickling through their fingers as they grasp its slippery texture before tasting it. Now compare this to offering them a plastic one. Think about the textures on your feet right now, possibly inside a sock and shoe; now think about walking barefoot through damp grass or cold, wet sand.

As children get older, think about how you are engaging them in the process of learning. What resources entice them to know, to understand or to recognise what they can do? When you set up your environment, are children free to touch, combine and experiment in different ways? Are they encouraged to share their ideas with others, perhaps with a group task or something too big or heavy to manage on their own? Can they adapt an activity to challenge themselves, taking risks and seeing how much further they can go today? Learning from mistakes rather than being put off by them.

As you spend time with the children, be careful not to dampen their motivations. At this age they are learning so much about their desire to learn, and when these desires are met with disapproval, you are effectively teaching them not to bother. Even when this means additional washing.

- Allow your children the time and opportunities they need to explore

- Let them experiment at their own pace, repeating and returning to things time and again as they refine their understanding

- Take the additional time to explore, rather than correct, allowing them to take more from a learning opportunity than the one way of doing something that you already had in mind

- Allow them to develop their social and communication skills with different age groupings; in a crowd, in small groups and sharing one-on-one time

- Offer varied opportunities within rich and varied environments full of open-ended opportunities where they can explore and experiment with their ideas, rehearsing and reinforcing their ideas through repetition

- Offer them the time and tools for the job, along with the permission and understanding to investigate, to manipulate and to try things out, just to see what will happen

And as you do so…

- Consider whether their touch, sight or hearing, or their sense of taste or smell are being engaged. Or could they be?

All the while considering the basic needs of a young child

First and foremost, be sure to value every moment of a child's early years, when so much of their foundational growth is occurring. Engage with THEM, rather than becoming overly concerned with the activity you had in mind. Involve their multiple senses and allow them to combine and adapt their experiences. Allow them time to process their thoughts and feelings, but also be aware of overstimulation by being in tune with their need for space and opportunity to blow off steam, to relax and just be.

And most importantly, ensure your children feel emotionally stable and secure. When they feel relaxed and at ease, within secure relationships and calm environments, they can turn their attention to all their other pursuits they need to engage with. Your children need you to understand more than WHAT they need to learn, they need you to understand HOW they are internally driven to learn. And how you are laying the foundations of this learning, now and for all their learning to come.

2 Connecting with young children

Communication, movement and play

As parents and carers, we want our children to develop in the best ways they can. For some that can mean wanting children to develop faster, but these two things are not the same. Children do need to accomplish a great deal, but when it comes to a child's development, faster is not better. In fact, faster can be much worse. Children need time to develop in all the mental, physical, social and emotional ways they need to before demands become overly focused, for example on learning letters or numbers. The best way for a child to access exactly what they need, when they need it, is through play.

However, our children are increasingly experiencing limited access to free play in their early years. And they are not the first generation to do so. When you ask many of the young adults caring for young children to recount their most enjoyed childhood memories, you are more likely to be told about consoles and nostalgic games of Pokémon, Mario Cart and Minecraft, than of den building in the woods. The trouble with this generational drop-off in free play is the deep impact it is having on the next generation's opportunities for and attitudes towards play. While no child needs to be taught how to play – they will make fun with the most limited of means – they do need permission. And if the gatekeepers to this play have not experienced the riches that it offers it does raise the question of how much they will advocate for it.

Play simultaneously embraces the multitude of learning styles that children need and naturally engage in throughout their early childhood. However, once in school, systems of lesson plans and the structure of the school day can see these natural learning styles becoming narrowly channelled. Add to this increasing demands for testing and achievement milestones and we are seeing many children disengaging from learning. If children are stopped from accessing suitable environments or are no longer given the time or social connections to engage, these are worrying times for the lost art of play, along with all the deeply meaningful experiences that play brings.

With every opportunity you have in the early years, it is then vital that you continue to offer every kind of play to children as you support and encourage their development.

DOI: 10.4324/9781003327042-3

"Accelerating" development is not the same as "improving" development. So, resist seeking to school them with overly academic approaches and avoid being enticed by the promises of flash cards or educational tools with young children. Instead, look to enrich children's learning in wider and deeper ways, rather than artificially seeking to propel them forward. And as you do so, support their interests, encourage their physical movement and cognitive reasoning and engage with them as you connect on every level.

Knowledge

Know the importance of communication, movement and play in the minds and bodies of young children

As children get a little older the ways in which they communicate change. No longer looking to the adults around them to take care of their every need, they are becoming more self-sufficient, more capable and more in tune with the things they want and need. Along with changes in their abilities and interests come adaptations to how they communicate and engage, both with their peers, which you will see as their style of play and connecting with friends develops, and with the adults around them (Figure 2.1).

Figure 2.1 As their methods of interacting and engaging with those around them are maturing, children need lots of opportunities to practice. Bringing children together to explore a common interest is a great way to facilitate this.

As their capabilities grow and their activities take on a more complex nature, the function of the adult within their development can become less clear. And without trusted knowledge and considered understanding, this role can fast turn to one of "instructor" if we do not remain mindful of the purpose of the early years and the tremendous growth and development that is occurring.

Communication

In previous books in this series, I have looked at how children's speech is developing. However, there is a huge difference in a child's ability to hear language and formulate words, to being able to communicate with others and the social skills required for conversation. These are complicated skills that are being rehearsed every time you see the absorbed face of a child being genuinely conversed with.

Learning to communicate through language is so fundamental to a child that they are practicing it from the moment they are born. From day one they will have been surrounded by language, learning the rhythms and tones and later the words and their meaning as they engage in the two-way exchange of communication. The more speech a child hears and the more opportunities they have to practice, the better they become at this process. Now, as their cognition is maturing and vocabularies are increasing, children need opportunities to interact in a variety of ways.

- Within language-rich environments children are given opportunities to trial their language

- When given a voice and a choice they learn the power of their words

- When you take the time to listen you show them their thoughts are worthy of your time

- When surrounded by novel opportunities they become interested in discussion

- When they are introduced to new words, they develop an extended vocabulary

- And when external noise is managed, they can hear the language being spoken by others

Through these moments of deep level engagement, you are developing the communication techniques that children will later depend on. This is of course essential throughout their education, determining how equipped and confident they are to engage in the school classroom, it is one of the biggest indicators of their success within it. But more than this, you are also supporting a child's mental abilities to flourish. You are developing their personal identity as they learn to express their thoughts and feelings. You are establishing their sense of self-esteem as they learn to value and embrace their ideas, rather than fearing them or assuming them unworthy of attention. And you are establishing expectations for how they will respond to future social interactions, including peer pressure. So, offer lots of linguistic input, plenty of chances to talk back in real and meaningful exchanges and keep the purpose of language and communication fun!

Movement

I am often asked about how much physical activity children should be receiving daily, especially now as they are becoming more mobile and are in greater control of where and how they will move. While we can consider various guidelines that are in place to advise this, we need to look far deeper than the clock on the wall. Physical activity is about much more than an allotted time frame in which to blow off steam. As I have explored in previous books in this series, its importance has repercussions throughout a child's mind and body and we must do all we can to encourage children to get more of it.

You may have seen headlines and social media reports warning that childhood obesity is perhaps the single biggest problem facing children in developed countries. This is a shocking statistic when you consider the health issues associated with being overweight and the fact that weight gained in childhood is typically retained and added to into adulthood as overweight children tend to become overweight adults. However, the sad truth is that our children are more inactive and unhealthier than they have ever been.

Unless they are sleeping, it is unwise for children under the age of five to be inactive for any length of time. The UK government suggests that between the ages of three and four, children should be active for at least three hours a day, spread throughout their waking hours. Now they are a little older, their physical activity will include a wider variety of energetic activities. And for at least 60 minutes of this time they should be out of breath as their hearts beat faster. As you talk with your children about the need for exercise, encourage them to look for these signs. Place their hand on their chests and help them to notice that they become sweaty as you increase their knowledge and awareness of their own body (Figure 2.2). All adults controlling the movements of children need to be aware of this and careful of the practices that are being modelled. And the best way to encourage this is through unstructured play. In contrast to passive entertainment, physical play encourages active movement and as we look to build active, healthy bodies with every opportunity, this can only support the resolution of the obesity epidemic.

Figure 2.2 Encourage children to see the effects of physical activity as their hearts beat faster and they start getting sweaty. Then help them understand why, along with why this is so important.

Play

In my work I am seeing more and more adults who seem to have lost the art of play. They come to me unsure of how to act, what their role within the play should be or concerned for when things did not go as expected. The first thing we need to know and remember about play at any age is that it is a cherished right of any child and an essential part of childhood. And when taken in its truest form, for all the years to come.

From the time they are born, children play. As they grow and develop, the ways in which they play will change, but this natural instinct remain strong. As a small baby they are inquisitive about their world, especially the humans in it and particularly their faces as they try everything to engage and interact. In their earliest forms of play children are investigating their surroundings and the objects within their reach, using these objects as if they are real by the time they are about 12 months old.

A little older, at around two or three years of age, children engage in "observer play" as they watch other children playing. Around three years old, this shifts to "parallel play". Now their observations are becoming quite intent as children mirror the actions of others. And as their play matures, "parallel play" becomes "collaborative play" as interactions increase and the play becomes more complex and involved. In fact, studies show that children may now spend more time in creative discussion, negotiating the rules of play than actually engaging in the play itself!

As play becomes more elaborate, it is used to explore concepts as a child's understanding and abilities grow. Whether it is time for a fairy's tea-party, or the dinosaurs are about to attack the knights castle, every social dilemma and facet of life is explored and better understood through play. This allows children to explore complex issues that they are not yet mature enough to comprehend in other ways.

Understanding

Understand how children's changing abilities and interests need to be nurtured, explored and be given the room to be set free

By the time children reach their fourth year, they may have been in the same environments for some time. Familiar with the opportunities, the resources and ideas, they may seem more than ready for something new. But with their next transition a little way off it can be useful to reimagine the environment and the experiences they are surrounded by.

With maturing abilities and increased physical, cognitive and social skills, the stimulation and freedoms they are surrounded by need adapting, inside and out. You can look to validate their increased levels of interest in the world around them by avoiding over-regulating their time or over-structuring their week. Instead, engage with them as you explore the concepts that have interested them. Provide stimulation if necessary and the tools as required and allow them to ponder and wallow. With freedom of movement, encourage them to access the resources they need with the time to lose themselves in their enquiries and show understanding as they explore their more mature ideas, feelings, emotions and behaviours.

Communication

When children play together, they are learning how to work in groups, to share, to negotiate, to resolve conflicts and to learn self-advocacy skills; all of which require and promote good communication. The more opportunities they are given, the more likely they are to participate, becoming involved in decision-making skills, moving the play onwards at their own pace, discovering their own areas of interest and ultimately engaging fully in the passions they wish to pursue. When children are given opportunities to engage in child-led play rather than activities being directed by adults, they develop their social skills as they engage, putting forward opinions and listening to and accommodating the opinions of others. The conventions involved here are not necessarily the same as conventional social interactions and must be experienced time and again as children develop their techniques. However, when play is controlled by adults, children tend to acquiesce to the adult rules and concerns and lose some of the benefits of this rich engagement that play offers them.

The developing level of a child's communication skills has a great bearing on a number of different functions. It is determining the ability with which they engage in conversations, asking for what they need. It is impacting their level of understanding, of all things going on around them. It is determining how well they are engaging with their peers and forming relationships, and it is offering them a sense of belonging as they engage with everything and everyone around them as well as opportunities to develop creative leadership and group skills.

- Now they are maturing, children need opportunities to push their limits, to be courageous and confident through different challenges

- When you invite them to use their imagination and their intuition, you offer them ownership of their environment and their place within it

- By giving them a voice, they can experience what it means to solve real problems and make decisions

- By allowing them to freely engage with the environment and those in it, they are learning about what they know and what they want to know

- By voicing their opinions, they are experiencing what they find interesting and satisfying

Within this communication-rich environment of play, children who start well will do well. However, the longer a child with limited communication skills continues to struggle, the more they will continue to fall behind. You need then to be aware of this and be taking active measures to provide the support that is needed.

Movement

Young children tend to have very high self-esteem. They will be quick to have something to say about most things. They will also want to have a go at everything and will probably be quick to tell you that they can run faster and jump higher than you! However, these impulses tend to decline as they get a little older and realise that there are others that are better. They experience what it means to fail and realise that there are lots more things they need to learn or perfect. So, while children are in these eternally optimistic early years, it is important to introduce them to a range of opportunities as they share opinions, engage in physical activities and experience diverse styles of social play as they develop an enjoyment in them.

While there is no guarantee that children will keep hold of any interests you develop in them now, it is certainly more likely than them discovering a love for physical activity after they have spent a largely sedentary early childhood, or of finding a voice when they have felt silenced – especially if this also means combatting issues that may have resulted from it.

When children experience a very sedentary childhood, rarely engaging in physical activity, they grow up having not developed a love for it. Or indeed an appreciation for the benefits that it brings. As they move from early childhood, they soon become self-conscious, concerned with their performance and being good enough in their middle childhood, or their appearance as a teenager. With links to body image and social acceptance, this tends to be particularly pronounced in girls who are less likely to embrace new physical hobbies for the first time. But therein also lies the good news. At a time when children are keen and eager to try almost any new experience, you can embrace this opportunity to try everything. These do not have to be expensive or involve elaborate equipment. But you do need to be mindful of the comments and behaviours that you are role modelling, especially when it comes to your expectations, to being outside or getting physically active.

Play

Through play children are exploring complex issues that they are not yet mature enough to comprehend in other ways. It allows children opportunities to create and explore in a world they can master, conquering their fears while rehearsing more adult roles. Common themes include getting lost and being found, being small and being powerful, facing danger and being rescued and dying and being reborn. These can all be explored in play as children work through the stressful or confusing events in their lives as well as things that are fascinating to them in ways that they can safely experience, allowing them to gain an understanding and the coping strategies they need to manage the real issue.

Play is now beginning to involve the understanding of some very complex rules, both those that are established and set within the game and those that are being discussed and altered moment by moment. There may be an element of "winning" and "losing", which may feel quite distressing for some. Unaccustomed to things not going their way, children may try to cheat or loudly accuse others of cheating. They may announce changes to the rules, blame others, quit or seek to end the game for anyone else playing. Play is a great way to help a child experience and work through these complex ideas that they will meet in many social situations.

Their play may also involve themes that appear aggressive, where danger or dominance are involved. Games that follow a "good guys versus the bad guys" plot line are not in themselves harmful and allow children to work through some complex issues that may be scaring them. If you become concerned about the levels of danger, dominance or aggression that are being explored, talk to children about what is happening. If their play appears to condone violence or dehumanise those being portrayed, help them to think about what is happening. How might this feel to the other person? If they have shot everyone, how will the play continue?

Support

Be supported in safeguarding this time as you explore children's tremendous potential, knowing that opportunities for rich, meaningful play will have far greater long-term potential than the achievement of any short-term goals

To simultaneously cater to all a child's needs requires well-planned resources and environments, both inside and out, preferably with free and instantaneous movement between them as their evolving capability for independent thought is facilitated and gratified. But to make deep and meaningful connections children need to touch and manipulate objects. They need to experiment with concepts, freely introducing and combining new ideas as these thoughts occur to them. Within the freedoms of the early years, consider how you can allow children to make mistakes with opportunities to try again, unafraid of demonstrating and celebrating their individual ideas. Without the pressures of a school curriculum dictating expectations or interrupting motivated play, connect with children on every level as you explore diverse experiences, supporting and encouraging all areas of their learning (Figure 2.3).

Figure 2.3 The joy of learning something unexpected in the moment can come from anywhere. With authentic provocations and your genuine interest, have fun learning and exploring together.

Nurturing communication

When communicating with children you need to remember that they are active and independent thinkers who learn best when allowed to combine the many different processes of learning. If you are listening properly to them, you will not need reminded of this fact. Given opportunities to explore their ideas they will take the logical steps they need to explore their lateral thinking. When they are supported to see something real come from something they have talked about, these connections in their learning are enhanced, making and adding personal relevance as they reflect on their past actions and achievements.

But this requires permission to access and repeat experiences when they need them and how they need them. So, listen for their requests for support before offering it or telling them what to do. And allow them to understand the world in unique and highly personal ways. All of these processes are an essential part of developing the diverse thinking and reflection required for symbolic and abstract thought and to the promote meaningful levels of understanding that go beyond surface knowledge. But access to these styles of learning may well be scarce in a formal school classroom, so make every possible use of them while you can.

Allow children to experience what it means to have a voice, possibly through the choices they are allowed to make, around the environment or the food they might like for a snack today. Rather than throwing the field open, you may decide on the nutri-tionally balanced snack you are having today, whilst offering some practical choices you can live with. Would they like carrot sticks or apple slices? One rice cake or two? Even if you know they are making an unwise decision, show them they have choices and how to manage a mistake when you put the second rice cake to one side, ready for when they tell you they are hungry before lunch time.

Nurturing movement

Children need no encouragement to move and be physical. However, they can be actively distracted from it. If this has been their experience, they may have forgotten the appeal of being active or need some reminding of the fun involved. With physical health strongly correlated to mental health, the habits that are being established in early childhood are the strongest indicator of physical and mental health as children develop into adulthood. If they're a stranger to activity during their earlier years, however, they are unlikely to embrace activity as they become older, as these healthy habits have not become a way of life. If you do not have access to outdoor space, start with a walk to your local park where you can play chasing games, climb the play-ground equipment and explore all that is on offer. If you are unable to engage in these pursuits yourself, arrange a playdate. No one plays with children quite like children do!

You can support their social play by introducing competitive games within a safe environment. Start with games where they play together yet compete against their per-sonal best. After that, try cooperative activities such as building a den or working out how to construct a bridge. The activities you offer to children then need to be some-thing they want to do. They need to be fun and match their interests, so be prepared to be flexible. Unsurprisingly, if you make a child do something, the potential benefits are not seen in the same way. While they are young, try to find things where success has more to do with the effort they put in, rather than attributes that are beyond their control. And if they are struggling with the social aspects, you might like to try physical challenges that pit their efforts against their previous attempts, such as throwing balls into a hoop rather than complex football drills. Can they get more beanbags in the bucket this time, can they jump further than they did yesterday?

When engaging in physical activity, girls tend to prefer chasing games, while boys will tend more towards rough-and-tumble style games involving wrestling and pretend fighting. Many parents and practitioners tell me they worry about this style of play; however, rough-and-tumble play is not the same as fighting, as it does not involve real anger or aggression and all children should be enjoying themselves smiling and laughing, not becoming upset. If in any doubt, ask the children, "Is everyone having fun?" If not, the play needs to stop. Done right, this style of play is an opportunity for stronger children to experience holding back, taking turns at chasing or being on top. They are not trying to hurt or dominate the weaker child – in fact, playing rough without aggression develops children's ability to inhibit aggressive behaviour.

Nurturing play

You may think you are offering stimulating, engaging environments to challenge your children's thinking. But do you observe where the children go and the resources they engage with when you give them freedom to choose their play? Carefully consider the opportunities you are offering and where you are offering them (Figure 2.4).

Figure 2.4 The only way to really know if the activities you are offering are hitting their mark is to look at the children using them. Are they engaged and excited by what they are doing? Are they deeply involved in a task, exploring and coming back again? Do they inspire conversation and negotiation?

■ How do children's responses differ between different cohorts of children?

■ How about your youngest compared with your oldest?

■ What about between the girls and the boys?

■ Do you know how much external influence is already impacting children's choice of play?

■ Can children access all the features of lifelong learning regardless of where they play or are practical skills only catered for in construction?

■ Are most social exchanges happening in the home corner?

■ Could an underlying gender bias already be affecting their choices?

■ If the areas promoting certain styles of thinking or ways of playing are only accessed by some, what are the others missing?

There have been studies to suggest that male dominance within certain industries is rooted in the toys offered in early childhood. By offering construction toys to boys when those areas of the brain were strengthened would certainly support a better understanding of the maths, physics and technology subjects these industries rely on, whereas little girls tend to be offered dolls and the home corner from a young age and dominate within the care industries. You only need to take a walk down the "boys" or "girls" aisles of any toy shop to see this in action. Identify any areas you think are receiving limited attention and talk with your children about an activity to address this. What resources and planning might you need? Be inspired by their interests and enthusiasms as you let them guide you.

I am often asked whether there are fundamental differences in the ways in which girls and boys will play. If you ever watch a group of children playing, before long you will probably see girls in the group becoming animals, fairies or princesses, whereas the boys are more likely to become superheroes or action characters; monsters, dinosaurs and knights may soon join, and they are more likely to engage in war play. That said, every social dilemma and facet of life is explored and better understood through play, often in ways that we might not see looking in from the outside, so if your boys always gravitate to the big pink wings in the play box, and your girls love the armour and swords, embrace this glimpse into their creativity and thought processes. The idea of being strong and powerful is compelling for all young children, as are concepts of magic.

3 Helping young children manage their emotions in a social world

Imagine what it would have been like if, as a child, you had learnt how to manage your emotions; if you could have calmed yourself during every moment you felt anxious and found a sense of balance whenever feelings of sadness, stress or anger overwhelmed you. How empowering would it have been as a teenager, with the ability to understand and manage your own emotions and to recognise and act positively when friends were in a difficult place?

In previous books in this series we have looked at understanding a child's emotions and outbursts. We then considered ways of helping a child to recognise these emotions during Stage One of establishing their emotional intelligence, and ways of supporting them as they begin to manage these emotions for themselves as they begin the self-regulation of Stage Two. However, emotions rarely happen in a vacuum. And now, as friendships are becoming increasingly important, we will look at helping children to understand emotions in other people.

As children become more socially aware of other children, engaging more directly with them in their play, the alliances that are being formed begin to hold greater significance. The games that are permitted and the social rules that govern them start to matter and the emotions that are roused can become rather more complex. As they are increasingly interacting with others, they are experiencing the social implications of an emotion and how their feelings are feeding off the emotions of those around them, driving their behaviours in ways that can become destructive or unacceptable without some careful management. And in addition to the effect this is having on their own emotional stability, children also need now to start considering the emotions and behaviours of others.

However, children do not yet have the understanding to see the "bigger picture" of their actions. They do not yet fully appreciate that these moments will pass. And while they are feeling big emotions surging through their body, they need guidance to show them that this need not feel quite so bad. In this chapter we will then look at nurturing

DOI: 10.4324/9781003327042-4

a child's development of emotional intelligence through Stages Three and Four as they begin to understand emotions in other people and learn to cope with the behaviours this brings.

Knowledge

Know how and when children develop the emotions required to manage in social situations, using this to manage your expectations of them

When it comes to nurturing children through all their stages of growth and development it can often seem like we have just got one thing sussed, then something will change and make us feel like we are back at square one again. This can happen when they have established a regular sleeping pattern and then become ill and nothing will settle them. This can also be the case when you think you are beginning to understand a child's emotions and outbursts.

When talking about the emotions and behaviours of young children you may hear it expressed that "They are a different child when you get them on their own". This is often the case when this means being apart from siblings. A child may be great at recognising the emotions they are having, even managing to stop themselves becoming too upset, rebuilding the fallen tower rather than throwing the bricks around the room as would have once been the case. But you enter a whole new playing field now as other children are becoming a more noticeable feature within their environment and friendships are becoming more important. But as we begin to explore Stages Three and Four of a child's emotional intelligence, it is worth reminding ourselves of a few emotional truths.

- Emotions are neither good nor bad, they just are

- We can all feel positive and negative at times

- No one else can make us feel; our emotions are our own

- How we choose to respond to an emotion, believe it or not, is also a decision we make for ourselves

Learning to manage their emotions

Children are deeply passionate about things and emotional outbursts can become all-too familiar before they have learnt how to regulate the strong emotions that are a part of growing up. If a favoured toy breaks, a four- or five-year-old may be distraught with grief. If another child broke the toy, even by accident, they may be furious and an emotional outburst be a hasty and familiar response.

As children are learning to take active control of their emotions, we need to help them understand what is going on inside their own bodies, to recognise their emotions as they learn how to manage them. But this requires permission and opportunity to feel, along with the support they need to name what they are feeling, without fear spiralling them into negative thinking-feeling cycles that can only escalate (Figure 3.1).

Figure 3.1 Sometimes, all that is needed is a reassuring word to help scary emotions we don't understand feel manageable again.

Once a child can recognise the emotions they are feeling, they then need to actively take control, working with both their conscious and their unconscious mind as they learn to stop their strong emotions from controlling them. And if this wasn't enough, they then need to recognise the behaviours and actions of those around them, reacting in positive ways to avoid the upset and fallout when friendships fall victim to emotional responses. Quite the tall order!

However, before children can understand and respond adaptively to another person's emotional experience, they need to be able to manage their own. This takes strategies of emotion regulation if a child is to regain control over their emotional state, allowing them to rethink the situation and focus on reasons to feel happy or calm, such as a time when the anger will have passed. These are all a part of Stage One and Stage Two of developing emotional intelligence that I explored in the previous book in this series, *Nurturing Toddlers*.

Managing difficult emotions can be a stressful experience for everyone, for the child as much as for you. But this is all a part of growing up and learning to manage our body's reactions and a child will not always get this right. But this is when they need you the most. A child is learning how to respond to every future situation through the experiences they are gaining, establishing predispositions to react in certain ways as self-perpetuating thinking and feeling cycles establish. If unmanaged, these can present all kinds of difficulties and challenges, with long-term effects on both the child and everyone around them.

They may experience difficulties concentrating or simply sitting still. They may have an increased impulsiveness or a tendency to 'drift', with clear repercussions on their schoolwork and time in the classroom. With almost one in five children around the globe experiencing some form of behavioural or emotional problems during childhood, medicated responses are drastically on the rise. However, before starting any course of medication, especially those that a child is likely to be on for some time, we must look to understand the underlying causes before seeking to mask the problems underneath.

Developing empathy

When children come together in social situations we can often hear comments such as "Play nice"; "Don't forget to share"; or "Let them have a turn". But when you really listen to the messages behind these comments and the mature expectations that they are rooted in, it is no wonder that children's behaviours do not automatically adapt to demonstrate the change in emotion that is being asked of them.

Recognising emotions in others and imagining how that person is feeling is all about empathy. While a child may be acutely aware of the emotions and behaviours that they are surrounded by from a very young age, and they may even feel deeply wounded by the actions and comments of others, their empathy is not in any sense developed until they are around seven years old.

There are then essentially three interwoven strands of empathy. These are all difficult concepts to grasp and they need to be seen, experienced and managed before they can establish effectively.

- Affective resonance – Recognising another person's emotions through their behaviours

- Perspective taking – Imagining how that person feels

- Compassionate motivation – Being driven to respond to those feelings in a compassionate way.

Affective resonance – When you spend time with someone who is feeling a strong emotion, you will begin to physiologically respond in the same way. Recognising the emotions of others and taking them on as your own is a human response that starts from a very early age. In one study, researchers caused mothers to feel stressed; then, when reuniting them with their one-year-old child, recorded the child's heart rate increasing to match their mums', even though the children had not been exposed to the stressful situation themselves.

Perspective taking – Perspective taking involves recognising the emotions you see in someone else and imagining how they must be feeling. But this is very dependent on the age of the child, so do not expect too much. A baby will react to your stress by seeking comfort for themselves; they cannot yet recognise that it is not them that is hurt. From one to two years old, they may offer help and comfort, but it will be the way they would like it. So, do not be surprised if your toddler brings you their teddy bear. Between the ages of three and four they are becoming more in tune with other people and better at understanding your emotions. By now they would know if you asked them, "What makes mummy feel sad?"

Compassionate Motivation – While the first two aspects of empathy provide us with the knowledge of another's feelings, this does not necessarily lead to empathetic behaviour. We might recognise and imagine someone's emotions, but whether we do something about it relies on whether we want to and whether we are capable of it. For this to happen a child needs to lose the blatant self-interest and egocentric motivations of their younger years. Only then can they become able to comfort, to share with or help others – provided they have experience of doing so. Once a child can recognise emotions in themselves and others and manage them in the moment, they are better able to handle difficult social encounters when emotions may be running high – a key component in supporting all the important relationships throughout every person's life (Figure 3.2).

Figure 3.2 Understanding how someone else is feeling and choosing to do something to help them are very grown-up displays of developing empathy and they need lots of opportunities to practice.

In studies, females typically score higher than males when asked how empathetic they are. However, when the electrical activity in the brain and physiological responses in the body are measured, these typically show no biological differences. This suggests that although males are as empathetic as females, they do not tend to recognise or admit it. In a culture that may be suggesting empathy is not a masculine trait, despite research showing compassion is anything but weak, we need to help both our boys and our girls to recognise the importance of empathy. Let them see themselves as compassionate through the opportunities they have to show compassion, surround them with strong and caring role models and avoid asking too much from them before they are ready, regardless of their gender.

Understanding

Understand the importance of taking emotions seriously as children learn to recognise emotions in others

While it is healthy and necessary to experience our emotions, continuously experiencing intense emotions is not good for any of us. When negative emotions continue unchecked, they can become more deeply ingrained and emotional predispositions or personality traits can establish. If this is happening to a child in your life, you might see an ingrained temperament such as a tendency to whine, to be quick to cry or quickly resorting to aggressive responses. Sometimes these behaviours and the self-perpetuating thinking and feeling cycles that can establish may be confused by a diagnosis of ADHD and the like, with medications all too quickly prescribed. In reality, they may be a response to feeling self-conscious, nervous or anxious to be perfect or possibly from a place of fear. By understanding how behavioural and emotional health problems develop in our children, we can better address these issues at a time when we can actively help children to manage them.

Framing the way we see the world

When we think of our emotions, we can often think of the more dramatic moments of change, such as the emotional response to good news or the devastation we may feel when something goes wrong. However, we are all experiencing lower-level emotions all the time, informing us of how we feel in the moment, letting us know whether we feel ok or if something needs to happen to create a change. The way we feel these emotions is also having a great impact on the way we perceive our environment and interpret the events of our day. If we start the day feeling anxious, we can soon feel like everything is going against us, with knock-on effects until bedtime. Not only do our emotions deeply affect our outlook, but they also translate to those around us, especially our children who are looking to us to offer a sense of emotional direction and a calming rudder to their less mature, often fraught emotions.

Children have been experiencing every emotion around them since before they were born. Every confrontation and every embrace and the effects these are having on them begins from day one. If you are feeling frustrated when a child needs you, you may model being short tempered and dismissive, informing not only the child's behaviours and emotions, but also their developing methods of managing them. If we can focus on the positives around us, embracing a happy emotional disposition, feelings of happiness can be constructively reinforced. And with the children around us responding to all the emotions they are seeing and feeling around them, this is worth actively considering.

Simply said, emotions are a natural, healthy and necessary part of growing up that we want our children to experience at the right time and to the right extent. Negative emotions are a very real part of this too, and children need to understand how to deal with their own negative emotions, as well as how to interact with their peers when they are experiencing them. But all of this does need careful understanding, guidance and support.

The danger of allowing powerful emotions to go unchecked

We all feel powerful emotions throughout our lives and there will be times when we feel angry. Trying to eliminate anger is neither possible nor desirable. Anger can be destructive, but it can also motivate us to change our circumstances for the better. Equally, happiness, joy and love are emotions every parent would want for their child. But to experience these emotions unquestioned and unchecked within some relationships could see them staying in a situation that they would be better off getting out of.

However, if a tendency to always react in the same way goes unchecked, a self-perpetuating cycle can be established. Every time a child experiences the same thoughts and emotional reactions, they become conditioned to that emotion, with less and less conscious control over the emotional reactions they slip into. If negative thinking repeatedly cycles into negative feelings, these destructive cycles will impact how a child thinks about and perceives future experiences. As this begins to affect the actions they then take and the person they are becoming, this simply becomes a part of who they are.

If you are predisposed to frustration you are likely to react to most situations with an automatically frustrated response. To override this takes a great deal of active mindfulness and a huge effort of will to act differently. However, unless patterns of behaviour are consciously changed, ideally before children are even conceived, you will pass these traits on to them, ready for them to pass them on to their own children. A predisposition to negative thoughts does not develop because of one negative emotional incident. However, over time, processes in the body establish a chemical continuity and an emotional predisposition is created, intensifying over the days, weeks, months or even years that it is left to reinforce. These patterns are laid down from our earliest experiences and inform all our future responses and we must be aware of them.

Recognising emotions in others without needing to respond in kind

Although empathy will not be well developed in a child until they are around seven years of age, early signs are visible from birth. You can see this from just a few days old when a baby will become visibly upset when they hear the cry of other babies. Studies have shown that, from a very early age, children experience similar patterns of brain activity throughout their emotional receptors to those around them. When

Figure 3.3 We develop our emotions best when we experience them together. Whether they are positive or negative.

they witness someone experiencing an emotion, these areas of their brain light up in similar ways to when they experience that emotion for themselves. A little older and the frustration, anger or jealousy expressed by another child may prompt some similar reactions in them. As the same negative chemicals flood their bodies, causing them to mirror some similar responses, they may also want to scream and cry, to throw themselves on the floor or begin lashing out verbally or physically (Figure 3.3).

Being on the receiving end of another person's feelings and responding in a compassionate way means letting go of the egocentric motivations of the younger years, something many adults still struggle with. But when you actively choose to have a calm response to things yourself as you engage with children, you can help them to stay in control of their own emotions, recognising them, naming them and laying down the brain structure that will inform their ongoing behaviours – provided you do not expect too much.

Recognising emotions in others and then using this to understand and manage the potentially irrational or hurtful things that are being said or done takes some very mature processes and requires lots of opportunities to practise within non-threatening or emotive situations. But once equipped, children are in a far better position to form and maintain healthy relationships going forward. While expecting mature, empathetic responses from children from a very young age is grossly misguided, there is much you can do to support their development. As you help children to identify, manage and control their emotions, helping them to understand what is driving their behaviours, you can teach them ways of not letting their emotions control them. And the best way of doing this will always be through play.

Support

Be supported in helping children develop emotional understanding, using it to make friends and play well together

When supporting children through the very real trials of what it means to feel secure within a social world, it is important that you understand the stage of social development that they are at so that unrealistic expectations are not in place. As a child develops both mentally and physically, they are experiencing many emotions. As a toddler they will experience frustrations that will engulf them when they cannot say or do what they are mentally ready for, missing their moment to engage. A little older and they will struggle to understand the mean things said by yesterday's best friend, while a teenager, with the rational part of their brain still seeing everything in simple terms of right and wrong, will struggle to understand your more considered "No".

As children seek to make friends and fit into a peer group, they must learn to manage their emotions rather than allow their emotions to engulf them. They need to understand what it takes to maintain a relationship through its differences of opinions and to understand that other people's words and actions may be coming from a very different perspective to their own. You can help a child to develop all of these skills through guided support, managed behavioural techniques and by effectively modelling responses to conflict. It also always helps to have techniques to fall back on, reinforcing positive outcomes every time you use them.

And it is here, with consistency and confidence, that you can support children, guiding them as they face difficult moments and sharing techniques that they, in time, can apply for themselves. Firstly, by preventing more dramatically emotional moments and then through supporting them as they develop through four stages of emotional intelligence. Stages One and Two, which look at supporting children to recognise their own emotions and then regulate them, were explored in the previous book in this series, *Nurturing Toddlers*. Now that we are looking at older children, these initial stages are no less important. However, with their growing social maturity we can now look to Stages Three and Four as we recognise emotions in others and manage relationships.

Stage Three: Recognising emotions in others

The third stage in developing emotional intelligence is rooted in recognising emotions in those around us and understanding what this is telling us about how they feel. This is linked very strongly to empathy, which, as I have mentioned, is a very mature process that children will not perfect for some time. That does not mean, however, that we should not be offering its foundations from this early age.

If we look again at the three strands of empathy we can see how to best support children in their development.

Affective resonance – Recognising another person's emotions through their behaviours
- Firstly, make sure a child's own emotions are not overwhelming them
- Work through Stages One and Two to help a child learn how to manage their own emotions
- Acknowledge how other people's emotions can make us feel as children build a foundation for empathy
- Play games to recognise and name the behaviours they see in books, on television or in those they see and the emotions that might be making the person act that way

Perspective taking – Imagining how that person feels
- Help children by openly talking about your own feelings
- Develop an awareness and curiosity in children about how other people feel
- Talk about the behaviours they are seeing and how the person may act differently
- Use friends, family, even characters in a book to talk about the emotions around them, imagining how a given situation must feel

Compassionate motivation – Being driven to respond in a compassionate way
- Once you have considered how someone might be feeling, talk about ways you could support them
- Model ways of supporting people in their life, modelling the actions you might take
- Consider the actions that are best suited. A visit to grandparents might be much better than flowers sent through the post. Helping pick up the bricks might be better than telling a friend they have missed one
- Help them to recognise how they could respond warmly to a friend's feelings and offer them opportunities to do so.

All the while, take care that all children's feelings and emotions are secure and that their well-being is nurtured. Only then will they be inclined to offer an empathetic response to others.

Empathy involves recognising the behaviours our friend may be displaying and understanding the emotions that could be driving them. A child then needs to understand what these behaviours and emotions are telling them about how their friend feels and to actively choose to do something about it. While recognising the emotions of our friend and adapting our own behaviours to them can be a hugely positive thing when playing with a group of close friends, it can also cause the play to disintegrate in an instant when you are not yet able to manage the complex processes going on. We then need to support children as they progress through these complex stages of empathy, rather than expecting it all from them at far too early an age (Figure 3.4).

Stage Four: Managing relationships

Once you have helped a child to recognise their emotions and manage them in the moment, they are better equipped to manage testing social encounters when emotions may be running high. The fourth stage in developing their emotional intelligence is taking all this empathetic development and teaching them to use it, supporting the key relationships in their life. But before supporting it, let's look a little deeper at what is happening.

Sometimes when we are faced with a very emotional moment, it can feel like we are both in the emotion and at the same time separate from it, almost as if we are looking down at ourselves. The part of you that is looking down at the situation is your frontal lobe. This is the part of the brain that enables your consciousness and supports you to achieve a state of balance once again. In these moments it can feel like we have no control because, as the brain detects what it thinks is a threat, it reverts to its primitive, subconscious parts. Rather than accessing the higher intelligence of the frontal lobe, it limits itself in this perceived emergency to automatic programs and instinctive responses. Whilst this plays an essential role in getting us out of the way of an oncoming car, we do not want to rely on this primitive part of our brain when our best friend has just said something mean about our drawing.

When children are immersed in emotions they are not fully equipped to understand, feelings of anger, hurt or hate can often be instantly expressed. By helping children to understand their emotions and the drivers of their behaviour, they

Figure 3.4 Children will often find themselves experiencing strong emotions they don't understand, whether these are their own, or fallout from a friends. Your words of reassurance are then key to helping put everything right with the world again.

can see them for what they are before irrevocable damage is done to a relationship. And if we can support a child as they learn to recognise and understand the emotions of others, they can then learn to manage the irrational and hurtful things that are sometimes said in ways that support burgeoning relationships.

1. Take a moment to breathe

   During a social encounter, children's immature brains can be quick to respond from the more primitive regions of their brain. Help children retain control of their higher intelligence by working with them to actively manage their responses and actions.

2. Take a moment to hear

   Practice taking a moment to help a child calmly hear what another person is saying when in an emotional situation. Remind them that sometimes we can all speak in ways we do not mean and consider the feelings that may have prompted what has been said or done.

3. Take a moment to think

   As you offer a child an opportunity to take a moment, model or suggest more considered responses to the situation while taking into account the feelings and realities that the other person may be managing. Think about more than one way of solving a problem, and consider how relationships need give and take and that our actions influence and affect all those around us.

Model this in the ways you interact with those around you and the choices children see you make. Show them and remind them how you have a choice over whether you continue with a negative emotion or actively seek to change it. As you develop this emotional understanding with children they can begin to recognise and manage their feelings and emotions for themselves. As we look at taking this emotional awareness into considerations of children's behaviour over the next couple of chapters, know that you are offering children methods for managing their emotions for life, methods that will be shown in the behaviours they display which can, in time, be passed on to their own children.

4 Supporting young children's developing behaviours

Childhood comes with so much to learn, and mistakes will be made. But it also comes with continual opportunities for learning. Yes, that is what the meltdown in the middle of lunch was for! We can see these moments as occasions to be feared and avoided or opportunities for growth. But this takes an understanding of the root of a child's behaviours and actions and the feelings that are prompting and directing them.

As surprising as this may sound, a young child's behaviour is not that different to your own. When you ask yourself why you cannot get a child to share their toys, to come in from the garden or to eat everything on their plate, ask yourself how that would feel if someone were asking it of you. Imagine if the chocolate bar you have been looking forward to all day now needs to be shared amongst a group. A trip out that you had been anticipating is prematurely cut short. Or you are asked to eat something you don't want or can even identify. When questioning the demands being asked of you, how would you feel if you were told to simply accept what was being expected, silenced despite your enquiry or compared to your neighbour? How frustrated would you feel at being controlled by those stronger than yourself or reprimanded for speaking your own mind?

While it is often the outward displays of behaviour from our children that prompt our actions, to understand this behaviour we need to take a step back and remind ourselves of what is at the root of them. And this resides in a child's feelings and emotions. Childhood comes with so many opportunities for a child to learn by and gain greater understanding – whether these are the lessons you would like them to be learning or not. And you need to grasp every potential opportunity, even if in more difficult moments, you feel like you would rather run and hide. If you try to ignore their early attempts at coping with their emotions, what learned behaviours are taking root? If you pretend it is not happening or manage it poorly today, ask yourself, what will happen tomorrow? And how many more of these opportunities do you have before they are managing their behaviours without you?

DOI: 10.4324/9781003327042-5

Knowledge

Know what happens to children when ineffectual techniques are used and the processes that need to be implemented

Managing your behaviour when you are in your early childhood is a tricky business. Not only are you trying to learn the behaviours expected of you, but you are also learning how to manage your body, your feelings and your emotions, all of which needs careful understanding from those around you, together with their informed guidance and support.

At every stage of this development a child is also looking to assert their individuality and their independence as they distance themselves both physically and emotionally from those closest to them. Whilst this can be difficult in the middle of a particularly fraught moment, this is all very natural and a big part of them growing up and understanding who they are in the world. It is not something you should be taking as a personal indication of your child-nurturing skills.

If you want a child to become a responsible, resourceful, and resilient individual you need to give them room to grow. And yes, at times to make mistakes. As often as they will fall when learning to walk, a child will make mistakes when learning how to behave. And before their behaviour can mature, a child needs to have developed a sense of personal ownership, a sense of who they are and how they should act in the moment. This takes many opportunities to try (Figure 4.1).

As we explored in early chapters and other books in this series, this inner sense of themselves cannot develop if all the control for their behaviours comes from

Figure 4.1 Some simple tasks that they are responsible for or expectations like hanging their bag up when they come in all help give a child a sense of responsibility and more importantly, a sense of belonging.

you. What happens when a child gets older and must make decisions regarding their behaviour and actions, perhaps under peer pressure, when a trusted adult is not around to guide them? If you offer them a bribe to eat their greens today, will it be expected tomorrow? And how much bigger will the bribe have to be to offer the same incentive?

Guiding children's behaviours

We've all heard it: "If you come in from the garden you can see the treat I have for you…. If you don't come in, you won't go out tomorrow!" Whilst bribes of great things that will happen if they do and threats of removing the fun if they don't may seem to work in the short term, they do not teach a child anything. Nor do they offer them any chance for growth. No punishment or reward ever gave a child a reason for continuing to act in a particular way when there was no longer the incentive to do so. That said, a child's behaviour does need guiding – but so much more productive than threats and bribes is the concept of discipline.

Disciplining a child is all about teaching them about the choices they are making and the consequences that come with them and this can start from a very early age. When we demonstrate concepts to children that are a very real part of everyone's life, they can experience the power this offers to them, not over them. It is a process that instructs and guides a child to act beyond compliance and expectation and instead to react from a place of empathy, integrity, and wisdom.

When a child is raised with discipline, they learn to see their mistakes as something to be rectified and embraced as a learning opportunity. Rather than being frightened of getting something wrong, it gives them ownership of their problems and helps them to find ways of solving them, while leaving their dignity intact. They learn from their experiences as they choose whether they want something to happen again, all the while leaving them more confident in their actions, rather than being afraid to try.

The impact we have on children through the messages we send

It is unsurprising that research shows that how the key adults around a child think and feel about others correlates with how that child will feel about the same issues. You may believe your children take no notice of the things you do or say, but they take everything in, even when you think they are ignoring you or are otherwise occupied.

■ Children who are surrounded by adults who are generally helpful to others are likely to be sensitive and altruistic to others, developing behavioural traits that will in time influence their own children

■ If a child hears negative comments about race, religion, gender or abilities, they are being taught a world view and social order that will readily inform their own

■ If on the other hand a child sees the adults around them stand up for the values they believe in, speaking out against injustice, they are more likely to transfer those lessons to their own everyday experiences

As a child establishes a sense of who they are, they will "Do as you do", far more often than they will "Do as you say", continuously looking to you to role model how they should behave in the world, as well as the beliefs and values they should live by. This is infinitely more powerful than if you simply tell a child to be nice to their friends, to take turns or to share their toys. This conformity between children and the adults around them seems to decrease through the teenage years, but it is clearly present in early and middle childhood. So be mindful of how and where you attach your strongest emotions, or the thoughts you have about others as it is this that will tend to surface. Even when you think you are keeping your views for when you are out of hearing, these opinions are influencing your comments and actions and as a result, how your children begin to view the world and the people in it.

And the methods we choose

Many common behavioural management techniques actually do more harm than good. As you are unlikely to be the only person caring for a child it is a great idea to have these conversations with everyone involved. The last thing you want to be doing is sending your children mixed messages, so it is important that everyone has a clear understanding of both the methods being used and the effects of them.

- **Negative reinforcements** – Sending a child to their room or to a "naughty step" to "think about what they have done" is effectively punishing through physical isolation. Refusing a cuddle for their misdemeanours uses emotional isolation and if you are making a point of verbally discussing their crimes, embarrassment or humiliation adds to the punishment. These negative reinforcements all seek to shame, degrade, humiliate or belittle a child.

- **Positive incentives** – Bribes and rewards are no better, as pointless cycles of emotional frustration are experienced over ever-increasing bartering systems. Rather than constructively teaching your child lessons they can build on, they are learning to ask, "What will you give me if I do?" These external motivations do not inspire compassionate, honest, trustworthy or even fair responses, they simply manipulate a child into performing a task.

By making a child dependent on rewards and external incentives, you effectively minimise the likelihood that they will develop a strong sense of themselves, able to control their behaviour and take responsibility for their actions. Instead, they learn to behave in a particular way simply for the payoff. And negative consequences can make them fearful or nervous to try.

Understanding

Understand what is driving children's natural behavioural instincts and help them to recognise these as you promote their effective choices

To understand a child's outward displays of behaviour, we must then take a step back and remind ourselves of what is at the root of them; their feelings and emotions. As I have explored in previous chapters and books in this series, feelings are neither good nor bad. They are simply motivators for the body, signalling the potential for something or acting as a warning sign that something needs to change.

In this way they cannot be right or wrong, they simply "are", and as such you are not looking to deny a child their feelings, but you do need to teach them how to take responsibility for what they do with them. In the same sense, other people cannot determine your feelings. No one can make you angry; they may provoke you or invite you to be angry, but you are in control of how you respond and you alone are responsible for the consequences of that choice.

Feelings – The body's motivators

For a child who is so often powerless within a situation, it can be difficult to choose how to respond when they do not feel in control; when they are not experienced in recognising or naming their emotions and they do not have a long history of experiences and consequences to draw on.

However, as a driver of their behaviour, you need to help children to do just that as you

- Teach them how to recognise their feelings

- While acknowledging their feelings as real and legitimate, and

- Without passing judgement.

Once this is achieved, you can begin guiding a child as they develop ways of purposefully managing the behaviours these feelings are motivating. When you help a child to see their emotions simply as warning signs that something needs to change, they no longer need to be afraid of becoming angry at a situation. You are not going to stop a child's emotional response from time to time, it happens to us all. But by accepting and taking ownership of their behaviour, they can learn to manage it, rather than have it control them. This can be a difficult lesson to learn, however, and one that children need a lot of support and practice in.

As children experience being listened to, loved and cared for, an important emotional stability establishes within them from which they can become more sensitive to the emotions of others (Figure 4.2). When you talk about a situation, you help a child to see the world through someone else's eyes and learn how to mentally take another person's perspective. In every emotional exchange you are then teaching a child about the importance of feelings, the trust you have in them to

Figure 4.2 When we listen, and experience being listened to, we can learn to regulate our emotions and become more understanding of the emotions around us. And this starts from our earliest experiences.

manage their own confidently and assertively and that they have your support and guidance should things be handled poorly. Only then can they, with experience and practice, learn to address their anger, fear or hurt.

Guiding – Not controlling – A child's developing behaviours

Guiding a child's developing behaviours is then an especially important and necessary part of nurturing children through their early years. Getting frustrated by their immature responses, denying them attention or activities for their mistakes or making an example of their misdemeanours is not. And this, essentially, is the difference between punishing a child's wrongdoings and teaching them when mistakes are made.

When a child is penalised, either by force, denying their movements or through put-downs or blame, an external force holds them accountable for what they have done. All the attention becomes focused on the captured behaviour and any element of choice in the moment is removed, as is any chance to develop appropriate, responsible or caring responses. What's more, if a child is expecting to be chastised for their mistakes, they will simply learn to avoid taking a risk or voicing an opinion. They are unlikely to push themselves or ask questions, resulting in behaviours that often lack creativity. These children will often resist opportunities to speak their mind, becoming submissive, compliant or sneaky. They are also unlikely to take ownership of their actions, meaning they do not understand the genuine consequences of them, or have the opportunity to fix what they have done.

When threats or punishments are given, power is removed from a child. This affects their sense of self-worth and self-dignity as they feel powerless to respond. There is no opportunity to develop an inner sense of right or wrong, nor a chance to willingly do the right thing. It teaches them nothing about why they have acted this way nor does it teach them alternative responses for next time; it simply teaches them to behave in certain ways when they are likely to be discovered and how not to get caught.

Whilst these techniques may seem to have some success in the short term, the job they are working at is getting a child to do what you want them to do. When you look beyond any short-term goals of compliance or making life easier in the moment, consider instead what your long-term goals are for a child. Would you not rather develop a child's capabilities and responsibilities and their capacity to think for themselves? Would you not prefer a compassionate, creative and competent individual with a strong sense of self, able to know when a situation or proposed response is not right for themselves?

Developing children's effective choices

It is true to say that our behaviours are influenced by the positive and negative outcomes we experienced the last time we tried something similar. This has then prompted behaviour management techniques that offer rewards for action we want to see more of and negative consequences given when we want children to think twice. While on the surface these techniques may seem to have some appeal, threats and rewards are short lived and have little impact when these interventions are no longer around.

Despite this, I have lost count of how many Rainbow Behaviour Charts I have seen and children's daily fight from the rain cloud to the sun. But think for a moment about how this seeks to affect a child. Imagine yourself in a new job where you are trying to learn the ropes and a boss who notes your every mistake and displays it on a chart for all to see. How would that constant, visible reminder feel? Or the confusion when you are not noticed for doing something that others are being praised for or are chastised for something you know others have done. I am always amazed by the perfect posture I see in classrooms when the stickers come out and the deflating sink that follows when one is not earned.

At best, this in itself is a blunt tool and teaches children little about the thinking behind the sticker. It also assumes that all potential behaviours are equally likely and significant, so it makes no difference what you choose to reward and this simply is not true. It also teaches nothing about why the chosen behaviour was right or wrong nor does it give children any motivation to do the right thing when the attention is not on them. For a child to behave in socially acceptable ways it involves them understanding what is expected of them and to have the ability, experience and inclination to do it. And this involves giving children reasons to change and the motivations to do so.

Positive reinforcement for good behaviour, while ignoring negative behaviours, is a part of this. But rather than bribes and rewards, research shows a smile, a hug or an encouraging word has far greater influence and continues to take effect even after incentives have gone away. Teaching children anything you want them to benefit from should be a rewarding, enjoyable journey, not something reserved for the negative moments. So, enjoy finding ways to connect with children and avoid any of the "What's in it for me" methods of point systems and sticker charts, or the physical and emotional exclusion of an ineffective time-out. While this can be an appropriate intervention to allow a distraught child the opportunity to calm down, no behaviour management technique should ever be used to punish.

Support

Be supported in guiding children's behaviours through the active steps you can implement, increasingly giving them ownership of them

A growing, developing child will be learning many new skills, some of which will come easier than others, and mistakes will be made. These should be viewed as part of the learning process. Given space, time and permission to experience their mistakes, a child can develop the skills they need to make better decisions, to manage their own behaviours and improve their social skills, ready for when adult guidance is not around. But this speaks of discipline, where mistakes are viewed as opportunities to learn and grow and where dignity is left intact.

Supporting children as they learn to manage their emotions and the behaviours they evoke is tough. It is then essential to have the knowledge and understanding of what is going on. On top of this, it is always reassuring and helpful to have a procedure to follow. Otherwise, you can find yourself saying and doing unconstructive things in the heat of the moment. You are unlikely to be consistent or have anything like a positive outcome. But with so many packaged procedures out there for you to purchase and follow wholesale, it is so important that you use the knowledge and understanding you have gained and think about what these methods are actually doing.

Influenced by everyone and everything around them

If you are struggling with a child's behaviour, firstly ask yourself some honest questions. Do they understand what is being expected of them? Is it within their capabilities? Always? Do you have clear, consistent and simple rules and expectations? Are they able to make active choices about the behaviours they are choosing? Knowing how to behave is complex, so to help children understand what is being expected consider how consistent the rules within your environment are and the behaviours the children are seeing and learning from. Children need opportunities to question and consider their own responses. They need to learn to recognise and understand what it is that they are doing, while making active choices. And they need to take ownership of that choice and to resolve any issues that have come from it (Figure 4.3).

Figure 4.3 Just as children learn about cause and effect through their physical actions, they are also learning the impact of their emotions. This can be a lot to unpick so some consistency as they learn these social rules are really important.

When you spend significant periods of time with a child in their early years you are becoming their most enduring role model. Through your conscious and mostly unconscious behaviours, your habits and reactions are imprinting on them, forming their behaviour through the examples you are setting and showing them how to manage their feelings by seeing how you think about and model your own. It is then so important that you demonstrate constructive methods of managing feelings with a child, talking things through in clear language that is accepting of mistakes and ready to resolve them.

When you:

- Show children how you work and play with others, being empathetic and emotionally available, you are role modelling the social skills these processes require

- Engage with children calmly, encouraging questions and not ignoring the difficult ones, you are teaching a child how to think, rather than what to think

- Arrange time for a child to be with different ages and generations, you allow them to share in the knowledge and wisdom of their elders while demonstrating what they know, igniting their spirit of curiosity while discovering the new

- Encourage children to listen to their own intuition, you allow them to be creative. Seeing the power of their own thoughts, spontaneous in their actions and inspired through their novel results, they can be creative, solving problems and thinking of the next step for themselves

- Consciously offer children lots of smiles, hugs and humour, they learn that love is to be given freely and unconditionally

- Spend time together, consciously avoiding questioning, directing or correcting them, you are building trusting connections and attachments between you

Turn a difficult situation into a valuable lesson

If a child is becoming upset at something that has happened, use this opportunity to work with them. Show them how they can actively change their focus and the emotions they are attaching to them as they alter their view of the situation. As you talk with the children about how the situation is making them feel, show them how they can actively take steps to go back to a state of calm, demonstrating constructive methods of dealing with emotional conflict.

But remember, children have so much to learn and mistakes will be made. And any negative behaviour should be met not with reprimands or bribes, but with natural and reasonable consequences that children learn are a part of life. All our actions and decisions have a direct cause and effect, but this is something children need to develop their understanding of before they are making big decisions or deciding who to follow without adult guidance. So, let them see that their decisions do have an effect, through natural and reasonable consequences that we all learn are a part of life.

Help children to see that we all get angry at times, saying and doing things we would rather we had not. The important thing is to not let our anger consume us. With their inexperienced and immature responses, situations may quickly spiral. Guide them as they develop the skills they need to choose their behaviours and learn to change either their attitude towards a difficult situation or the situation itself, and to avoid striking out at anyone and anything that happens to be nearby. The choice of behaviour is very much theirs.

- **The lead-in** – When you see a child becoming upset or frustrated, notice what is happening and help them to take ownership of their feelings.

- **The early stages** – Remind them that these feelings they are having are their own and they can choose what they do with them. Work with them to understand what is causing their frustration. Help them to address the issue, remove the problem or alleviate the situation quickly if they can.

- **When others are involved** – Support them to be direct with any individual who is evoking these feelings. Remind them that no one can make them feel angry, that their feelings and their responses are their own. Help them to communicate what they want or need, remaining open to other perspectives on the situation as you take care to avoid any angry feelings towards one another or the assigning of blame. Instead, help them to express their feelings clearly and directly as together they negotiate an agreement everyone can be happy with.

- **The fallout** – To support children in taking active ownership of their behaviours, they also need to be aware that behaviours come with consequences. These teaching moments should be a learning exercise to help a child see what they have done, to give them ownership of the problem and the opportunity to learn from the experience.

- **Facing the consequences** – These should be **reasonable, simple, practical** and a valuable **learning** tool. If toys have been thrown all over the floor it is **reasonable** that the mess is cleared up. The toys **simply** need to go back into the playbox. It can be **practically** achieved (this should not take all day or get in the way of everyone's play). It is used as a **valuable learning tool**, teaching children that if they do something they should not, their actions need rectifying.

Avoid becoming focused on the negative actions; try to notice all the good children are doing too: "You tidied your toys, now we have time to share a book together". Or find opportunities to offer them an encouraging response: "Look at the cereal on the floor, now you will need to get the dustpan and brush and clear it up". As you talk with them about their behaviour, help them to think about the choices they are making and the consequences of them. Then follow

Figure 4.4 Smiles and recognition for a job well done goes a long way!

this up by explaining why you want them to behave in a certain way, even if it goes beyond their current understanding as they learn to expect a consistent, yet fair response to their actions (Figure 4.4).

Children surrounded by opportunities to frequently engage in these kinds of conversations have shown significant benefits. When they are given the opportunity to discuss what they think should happen and why, they are better at engaging in empathy-based reasoning for themselves and more likely to engage in these prosocial behaviours. With this understanding in place, we can now look at constructive methods of managing confidence in these behaviours in your children, developing the ability to positively express themselves with techniques they will rely on throughout their life.

5 Developing young children's confidence to think and express themselves

When a child was born, they had no understanding of themselves as a separate person. They were not yet able to differentiate themselves as somebody separate from the others around them. To develop this individualised sense of being someone different is something that happens over time as we develop the mental, emotional and behavioural functions necessary to see ourselves as a separate person. As we develop this sense of being somebody different, our awareness of who we are develops and we begin to realise that in some ways, we are different from the others around us; our hair may look different, we might speak differently or be able to do different things. Then, as we effectively begin to manage our bodies and respond to our basic needs and drives, we establish a growing confidence in ourselves as a person.

By allowing our children opportunities to do things for themselves, feeling what their bodies can do, managing their environment and selecting their own goals, they develop this sense of personal power, of self-esteem and resilience. Opportunities to engage with other children and adults within wide-ranging social and environmental situations allow these skills to flourish, but also place a child in a position of comparison. What can they do compared to those around them and what do other people think of them when they do?

When children are given opportunities to see what they are capable of, they can experience what it means to persevere through a challenge and to shine. They develop a good sense of who they are and more importantly, a belief in themselves and who they might become. They are more likely to try new things and they tend to bounce back quickly after difficult experiences or failed attempts. One of the greatest gifts you can give to a child developing through these stages is then the ability to think for themselves. However, this does not come from seeking to make them think as you do.

While some decisions and responsibilities will need to remain with the adults around them for some time, take a moment and consider the decisions that are made for your children and your justifications for them. Is this a part of being a wise and caring adult

DOI: 10.4324/9781003327042-6

(everyone must walk, rather than run down the stairs) or am I afraid of losing my control (I get to pick who is at the front)? When you encourage children to think openly about what they are doing, they can gain the confidence to express their ideas as they develop. When they are allowed to make their own decisions without judgement, you empower them through a sense of responsibility. And as they see the results of their decisions, they develop the abilities to connect cause with effect and their actions with potential consequences – even when this comes through mistakes and unfortunate choices as they learn how to take responsibility.

Knowledge

Know the importance of promoting children's abilities to think for themselves and the impact this will have on them in the years to come

From a very young age a child is learning how to think. As a baby they were learning about object permanency; the idea that things do not disappear just because they can no longer see them. This is why peek-a-boo is so much fun. They are learning about the physics of gravity, which is why dropping things off their highchair never got old. They were recognising facial structures, the difference between male and female voices and the amazing knowledge that it is their thoughts that govern their actions. Children are then born thinking, seeing and hearing right from the start, but this depth of thinking capability needs stimulation.

Now that they're a few years older, children need a different form of guidance as they develop their ideas and thinking within age-appropriate freedoms. When children learn to make age-appropriate and meaningful decisions, in an environment where they can constructively work through their problems, you are teaching them to be responsible, resourceful and resilient. When they feel able to think for themselves, to know they can express these thoughts and develop their understanding with your guidance, you are teaching them complex social skills. Demonstrate how you too can express yourself with tactful integrity, modelling these techniques to your children.

Growing up is all about having our own thoughts, experiencing our own choices and the consequences of them as we learn and grow through them. However, children are not little adults and our expectations of them need to match their developing capabilities. When you realise that empathy is not developed in a child until they are seven years old and not fully until they are in their 20s, young children's squabbles over a strength of will are put in a whole new light.

Even into their teenage years, children are moving through fluid and malleable processes as they grow into the person they will become. Comments and actions of well-meaning adults can easily be misinterpreted, creating distortions which, if continuous, can impact their well-being in the moment and if prolonged, even their developing personality. Throughout all stages of development, it is then essential that we retain realistic expectations of our children, of their developing maturity, their capabilities and their intentions.

Feeling competent, confident and worthy

It is then key that we support our children as they establish their abilities to think for themselves, to have confidence in what they are doing with a good sense of where their competences lie and where new ones need strengthening, all the while retaining a sense of being worthy purely for being them, with nothing to prove (Figure 5.1). But what does it mean to feel competent, confident and worthy? I explored these concepts in the first book in this series when I looked at "Helping children feel competent, confident and worthy". So, for now, let us have a quick recap.

Figure 5.1 Feeling confident that I can do this, reassuring myself that I am still able to and feeling great about it when I see your smiles for my efforts.

Competence – The ability to do something successfully
To feel competent, a child needs to be able to see something through to a successful conclusion, no matter how small. To see how they can achieve this, they need to develop mental thought processes and the ability to think for themselves. They need a degree of emotional stability so that they can understand the emotions they may feel along the way, along with the ability to manage them. And they need verbal skills so that they may express their thoughts, wants and needs using their words. Once all these things are established and with lots of opportunities to practice, a sense of empowerment develops, with every experience feeding into the way they behave and respond to others.

Confidence – Having the belief that you can do something successfully
Self-confidence is a child's faith or trust in their ability to do something. All about past experiences, confidence is fuelled by every success they have experienced and is dented when things go wrong. This explains why young children sound so confident when they tell you how they will beat you in a race or perform cartwheels well beyond their means; they don't have much experience of not being able to. Their confidence will build as you allow them to make memories of times they do things with ease and when trying again paid off. If they begin to doubt their confidence, allow them to simply try again so that positive outcomes, even the little ones, can follow this additional effort. And take care to resist the negative feelings following setbacks or difficulties from

denting their confidence as you build up their resilience. This is an area I look at more deeply in the next book in this series when we look at "Developing nurturing methods of encouragement and self-motivation".

Worthiness – Feeling good enough

Worthiness is rooted in our values; our beliefs about what is good, what is right and what is important and how we ourselves measure up. These are very complex issues and yet are continuously communicated to our children, both when we mean to and when we do not. So, we must be mindful of the messages we are sending. Avoid comparing one child to another with comments like, "Look how nicely the girls are sitting" or "Buttercups did the task so well." All this does is help one child to take an instant dislike to another, while comparing their own skills only to find them somehow lacking. This is even worse when the example is an unreasonable ideal that their developing minds, bodies or social skills are not yet ready for.

Nurturing the development of a thinking child

Research[1] in the United States asked 1,600 parents of birth to three-year-olds how much they thought their child was aware of and how conscious of their feelings they thought they might be. Seventy percent of parents with six-month olds were not aware that their child was experiencing feelings such as sadness or fear and 65% did not realise that their child was also picking up on the impact of their own feelings. From the time a child is born, provided they are awake, you can be sure they are aware of their surroundings and processing everything that is going on. While they may appear completely dependent, helpless and incapable of most things, they are continuously absorbing all the world has to offer and trying to make sense of it. And these experiences are laying the foundations of a child's expectations of the next experience.

However, while a child is absorbing all these cues from you and the world around them, they have a very different way of processing them. Simply by virtue of their age and their experiences, children will have a quite different way of looking at the world than you do. They are driven by different desires, informed by a different agenda and with a very different understanding of time, empathy or consequence. We need then to be aware of our expectations and mindful of the impact these early experiences are having on our children.

We want our children to take in the wealth of information around them and, together with a deep-rooted knowledge of themselves, be able to make their own decisions, mindful of their level of competence in the task they are about to undertake and confident of being able to give the additional effort that might be required, all the while knowing what is worthy of their time and attention. But to do all of this successfully, children also need an understanding of the potential consequences of their decisions. So, even though they may not always make the decision that we would choose for them, they experience making them within a protected environment where they are safe to make mistakes as they develop an understanding of potential outcomes. This is not something we can teach our children; we simply need to support and validate their experiences of it.

Understanding

Understand the experiences and opportunities children need to develop their abilities to think and to express the thoughts that they have

Albert Einstein used to talk about imagining travelling at the speed of light when he was a child, using these ideas to base his initial theories of relativity. As parents and educators it is important to put our minds back and remember what it was like to be a child, experiencing the world for the very first time, seeing reactions you cannot read, hearing language you don't fully understand, being compelled to reach out and grasp at things just to see what it feels like, discovering what your body can do and trying to do the same as a friend. Children need time to absorb all of these experiences. They need opportunities and permission to use and develop a creative imagination, to have an opinion and make decisions as they develop a sense of ownership, consequence and possibility.

Developing confidence within themselves

Children are growing and developing through every experience, every day. Some of this growth is visible, but much of it is deep rooted, affecting the ways they think about themselves and the world around them. It affects how they consider themselves to be measuring up, both in your eyes and in the eyes of those whose opinion they think matters. And from this, they will be considering the degree of recognition and respect they feel they are deserving of. With greater access to social media and with concerns regarding child mental health increasingly on the rise, now more than ever we need to be mindful of the messages we are communicating and the opportunities we are offering.

It is then so important that we allow our children to feel competent through the tasks they perform and complete for themselves. In the early days this will undoubtedly come with some frustrations, but do not let their confidence become dented. Instead, give them the words to talk their issues through with you. Let them see their small victories, rather than becoming discouraged when they are on their way to achieving a bigger goal. And remind them of all the things they have achieved along the way, especially when, like in this moment of struggle, some extra effort was required.

When you offer children opportunities to experience what they can do, you can build confidence in their abilities, drawing their attention to these successes and supporting them as they find the words to talk them through. You can start small as you notice the victories that are important to them together, even if this is not quite where your focus tends to be. By drawing their attention to these moments, you are making these lasting memories more powerful and giving them a stronger voice to express them. As you do so, you can be careful of the value you unintentionally attach to things by the language that you use (Figure 5.2).

Widening their experiences to broaden their mind

When we become busy, we can forget that we are not simply taking care of children in their early years – feeding them, entertaining them and keeping them clean while we wait for them to grow up. They are already thinking, feeling people from the first day we meet them, influenced by every engagement, interaction and response they are surrounded by.

Figure 5.2 Children are surrounded by the actions and achievements of those around them and it is human nature to compare what we can do with others. So focus on their efforts, rather than their successes, as you build a child's confidence for what they can achieve.

When we show them what we find interesting, we encourage their interest in the world. When we explain what we are doing, we show children that they are worthy of our time and interest as we share our knowledge with them. And when we invite them to discuss and deliberate with us, we send the message that their thoughts, views and opinions are interesting and worthy too. Even though they may not fully understand the content, they are learning so much from these engagements, understanding from your intonation that you are considering your actions and making conscious decisions that you are in control of.

When children see you interacting with other adults, you are demonstrating the more mature social exchanges that are a part of the social world they are living in from your tone of voice, the gestures you use and the displayed emotions you model as you smile, contemplate, become enthused and reach conclusions. You can also model how different ideas can come together and result in new directions that were not possible alone. All of this is telling them so much about how to express the thoughts that they themselves are having and how to be a part of an exchange of ideas, a very real part of the social world that they will grow up to be a part of.

That said, there is growing concern that many children in the modern world are increasingly spending much of their time doing the same activities as each other; playing the same screen-based, preprogrammed games. With a child's brain being wired through every experience, these limited opportunities are causing many to fear for the eventual outcome. Will this result in a generation of children incapable of original thought or creativity? Where will they find any deeper meaning if they have no experience of searching for it?

An environment in which to think

Offering children a voice and with it, a sense of responsibility, is something that is embraced by the Montessori method from a very young age. From the time a child begins at a Montessori setting at around two and half years old they are given at least some responsibility for maintaining the orderly space they find themselves in. Purposefully designed with child-sized furniture and space to sit, crawl, and "work" on the floor, decoration is intentionally muted, making it easier for children to focus their attention. Quiet, peaceful and uncluttered with no electronic toys or screens, the room is full of interesting things to do. This can be quite a change to many homes or settings that can become packed full of as many toys, dolls, trucks, dressing up, books and games as possible. And the child, somewhat lost and bewildered in the middle of it all, is insisting that they are bored.

Sometimes we all need an environment in which we can hear our own thoughts; where we can explore the one idea we can hold in our head at a time with a degree of focus, together with the freedoms and lack of expectations that enable us to fully explore something before looking for additional stimulation or support if and when we need it.

By carefully staging an environment where children can select their own direction, they can experience what it means to follow a train of thought. With resources available to match their current stage of development, interests and desires, they can explore these thoughts in meaningful ways, accessing what they need, when they need it as their understanding or interests develop. And as they encounter problems or unexpected outcomes, they have the opportunities they need to acknowledge, own and solve these problems for themselves with the confidence to think they are capable enough to do so.

Within an environment where children have a degree of autonomy, they are then able to access the resources and experiences they need. Neatly arranged and spaced to be accessible, the children can be shown how to think about what they need, to access it freely and utilise it with minimum intervention. Through these experiences children can develop confidence in their own abilities. With some encouragement, they can learn to talk about what they are doing and why. And with opportunities to share and explain their journey, they can develop a sense of their own voice (Figure 5.3).

When children encounter problems, as they will do, you can show them that you believe that they can handle this. When you help them to talk through the issues or concerns they are having, you can show them you have faith in them, provided you allow them to experience some problems and struggles for themselves and share in their successes at the end of the day, no matter how small they may seem or how unexpected a place they may have come from.

Figure 5.3 Challenges come in all shapes and sizes and you may not be aware that grappling with the laws of physics is really important in this moment. However, having resources, and your genuine interest, always available goes a long way.

Be supported in ways you can help children to find their voice; to learn from their decisions, thinking more deeply the next time

Teaching a child how to find their voice and be assertive in offering their thoughts and opinions is an important skill that will benefit them throughout their life, supporting their relationships, helping them to say no to something that is not right for them or giving them the tools they need when they have something important to share. But to do this they need to develop the ability and the confidence to do so. However, life with young children can be chaotic. There always seems to be a reason to rush children, bypassing important moments of reflection. But these moments of sharing what another person is thinking or feeling can set you up with a mindset that will benefit the rest of your day.

Our behaviours around children will also have a demonstrable impact on how they behave. Copying the behaviours they see modelled around them, as well as the withdrawal or assertiveness you see them display, and the moments you take to share opinions, to listen to each other and invite them to think deeply about things that matter are then a significant part of this process. In these moments children are learning to find their voice and their belief structure. They are also developing listening skills and the ability and confidence to voice and assert their own views.

Learning language

Children will learn both the main language spoken in the home and any additional ones far more easily when they are young. And children learn this language by being surrounded by it. Whether they are learning their first, or subsequent language, this needs to be a two-way exchange and cannot be done through the passive, one-way experience of watching a screen. In fact, there is no clear evidence to suggest that casual exposure – watching an infant-targeted language DVD for example – has any positive impact. Children also need encouragement to speak language, to use it in novel ways, and to experience the range of associated gestures and facial expressions with opportunities to use more familiar words to fill in the gaps.

While certain aspects of language, such as grammatical rules and key vocabulary, are learnt better by older children and adults, motivation is key to learning anything – and young children have this in bucket loads, seemingly able to learn language without being explicitly taught. Young children also benefit from skills we lose as we move from childhood. In fact, evidence from families that move to a foreign country suggest that whilst the parents may start better, the child is soon hearing the mistakes the parents cannot hear, utilising synapses we have lost in adulthood.

Learning a second language

Studies show children who learn a second language enjoy a variety of cognitive benefits: improved memory, creativity and flexible problem-solving abilities. This does not need bilingual parents or major commitment to intensive training. Relatively small exposure to and use of a second language, regularly and over time, can be sufficient to reap significant benefits.

Children growing up in a bilingual household will typically learn to speak a little later and with a smaller vocabulary. With fewer words, they also tend to speak in shorter, less-complex sentences. This used to be thought of as a delay in development that should be avoided but is now thought of differently. Children rarely mix up their vocabulary, the rules between the languages or how or when to use it, all of which points to more flexible brains, capable of switching between tasks, increased working memory and cognitive processing, all of which have been linked to improved results in school-based tasks.

Finding their voice

As children develop their voice, they need to trial it and get instant feedback on how they are doing. So, look to envelop children in rich language opportunities and enjoy the fun and the benefits that communication and sharing in their thinking can bring. Where you can, follow their curiosity and current passions, particularly when they are something new as you give them this opportunity to share something novel with you. Listening and noticing what they are trying to share is an important place to start as you allow them to be the expert. And if this is an area you are not familiar with, use this great opportunity to share the opportunity to find out together. Use books and, where you can, real experiences as well as technology to share in their interest.

Thinking more deeply

Help children to think more deeply by considering questions and problems that require reason and explanation. When you are sat down together, perhaps over a meal, invite conversations that encourage them to think and to consider the opinions of others (Figure 5.4). "Is it right to lie if you know the truth may hurt someone's feelings?" "What makes a person brave?" You might also like to reflect on topics such as "What have you learnt today?" "Something really surprising happened to me today" or "What has been the most surprising thing someone ever said to you? Did it make you change your mind?"

When you are talking with children it is important to ask open-ended questions as you think of responses together, rather than the

Figure 5.4 Bringing children together offers great opportunities for sharing thoughts and ideas which you can then take further. This is so much richer than asking for an expected response – for everyone involved.

"I have the right answer" approach that children can sometimes experience from adult questions. You can encourage this with openings such as "I wonder why..." or "Have you ever noticed that..." and be curious about their thoughts: "Where did you learn that?" "How did you think of that?" or "That's really interesting, can you tell me more?" Throughout these exchanges it is critical that you leave the appearance of judgement behind by being careful about how you phrase your questions, avoiding provoking a child to feel on the defensive.

When you have shared views in this way you can take children's thinking even deeper by turning it into an informed thought, by helping children to find the information that backs it up. Combining thoughts and feelings and developing them with critical reflection and fact is all a part of establishing executive cognitive functioning and the ability to make reasoned decisions, with benefits throughout life.

Learning from decisions made

Begin by offering children choices early on. Strawberries or blueberries? Which book before lunch? Bricks or train tracks? These may seem like simple choices, but they can help young children get used to choosing, to speaking up for what they want and having a voice. As you then engage your children in the thinking process, encourage their reflections. But in doing so, consider how you and they view their mistakes or perceived mishaps. Is there any negative talk of getting things wrong, failing or not being good enough? Or can you take this opportunity for learning about constructive feedback, thinking about how they might do things differently next time, learning from what happened today as they see it as a valuable experience. Whilst the former will help construct a negative spiral, reinforcing a sense of inadequacy with any future set back, the latter will allow them to take this setback as a call to arms, helping them to see where they can learn more within what is an ongoing journey.

And always avoid the "I told you so" approach. This does little more than foster quiet resentment. Instead of "If you had put your coat on like I told you, you wouldn't be cold", notice when they are shivering and mention that "You look cold, honey." This simply allows them to consider how to respond and offers a memory for them to act differently next time. Provided they are not about to get hypothermia, avoid becoming locked into a power struggle that you know you will lose; in that instance, a child would rather freeze than suggest you were right.

Model by example

Use moments during the day to model decision making, thinking about its outcome and reflecting on what you may do differently the next time. This is a great way to help show children that we all have various options in front of us and decisions need to be made; that no one has all the answers and sometimes mistakes will be made. But despite this, it is ok to be assertive and speak up for what you want, without feeling like you might hurt someone's feelings, or indeed have your own feelings hurt. You might like to tell someone that you think differently about something in front of the children and model a discussion that, tactfully and respectfully, discusses this difference of opinion while respecting theirs. You can share past experiences with the children or choose a story that features a plotline similar to something they are themselves experiencing. This helps children to realise that they are not alone, that even adults struggle sometimes and that things tend to work out ok in the end – even if there were a few bumps along the way.

Note

1 https://www.zerotothree.org/resource/national-parent-survey-overview-and-key-insights/

6 Nurturing young children as they develop social skills

Throughout a child's life they will want and need to be social, to manage in social encounters, to engage in relationships of all kinds and to manage within this social world. This will involve having good communication skills along with the ability to use them effectively. They will need to engage with others, to be productive and contribute in harmonious and enjoyable ways. They will need to learn how to build successful relationships, both in the dynamic of the family, as well as with peers and with friends, colleagues and strangers. They will need to learn how to make their point understood, whilst avoiding unnecessary conflict as they develop methods of cooperation and understanding as well as learning to lead and follow within group situations. And for some children, much of this is not an easy process.

And yet, for a young child who is just learning to find their way in the world, their developing social skills offer them a way to communicate the needs they are otherwise powerless to have met. It is their way of being included into the group, essential for their survival and for learning from all the others around them. As they engage in these complex processes, mistakes will be made and guidance will need to be followed, whether this is desired or not.

All of this needs practice within nurturing and diverse experiences as children develop their communication and social skills over a lifetime of experiences. But social skills are about more than being able to have an interaction. Teaching a child to help, to share and to support others has many positive outcomes. When we are driven by a concern for the well-being and rights of other people, to feel empathy and develop caring relationships that benefit others, not just ourselves, we tend to receive that help back in kind. In fact, we do so well as a species because we are able to work together in ways that other species cannot. How else could we bring trades together to build great structures, to unite diverse specialisms to invent and produce, as well as forming clubs and organisations that entertain and support one another? It is then so important that we nurture the social skills of our children in all the ways that we can as they grow and flourish through the social encounters all around them.

DOI: 10.4324/9781003327042-7

Knowledge

Know the social skills children need to develop and the steps that can be taken when things need a little guidance

From the time we are born we depend on the connections we have made and the connections we are able to make with those around us. As a species we are completely dependent for a long period of time and to survive we need to have effective social skills to secure the care we need from others. Our survival depends on it. Without the ability to bond with others and to convince them we are worth caring about we would not be fed, kept warm or nurtured in any way. And our attempts at becoming a part of this social world begin from the moment we come into the world.

An infant will begin fine tuning the techniques they use to encourage attention from their first days and weeks, from seeking out faces in the images they see around them, to responding to the smiles and facial gestures that those faces pull. They will perfect the ability of gaining attention and of being able to keep it, of obtaining the responses they need when they need them and of developing the warm secure feelings that follow. Their social skills are so important to this sense of security that the areas of the brain involved in it are one of the first areas to develop. But social skills are about more than being able to interact with the people around you (Figure 6.1).

Well-developed social skills support a child's growth and development in a multitude of ways. Being able to understand and manage their emotions, to navigate conflicts as they arise, and to cooperate and work together all allow children to build stronger connections, allowing them to interact with ease and to be more likely of being accepted by their peers, with immediate and lifelong benefits. But the research also suggests that children with well-developed social skills early on tend to be happier and even do better academically, perhaps because once this basic human instinct has been managed, their attentions can turn to other things, but also because it has so many knock-on effects into all other areas of learning.

Figure 6.1 We are all fundamentally social creatures and our friendships and relationships are important to us throughout our lives. Here is where we are learning how.

Developing empathy

An important part of making and keeping friendships going, both in the short and the long term, is in understanding another person's needs. Putting the needs of someone else first, helping another person simply because it is the right thing to do speaks of "altruism". But is this ingrained, or somehow genetically encoded? Are we motivated to do this or is it something we need to learn?

Whilst altruism has traditionally been associated with maturity, certainly not associated with toddlers, research is now causing us to think otherwise. In one study,[1] an 18-month-old child was sat in a room on the lap of their parent. The mother was briefed on what was about to happen but told not to do anything to influence the behaviour of their child. After a minute or so, a researcher walked into the room carrying a large pile of magazines. Visibly struggling, they try and fail to open a cupboard door in an attempt to put the magazines away. In most cases, after watching for a few moments, the child will jump down from the parent's lap and go to the cupboard and open it, even overcoming their anxieties around a stranger to do so. So, is altruism a basic instinct from very early on that we simply need to keep hold of? Are children predisposed to act in this way, possibly to invite social connections and friendship?

While it is one thing to realise the feelings of another person, this does not necessarily lead to empathetic behaviour. We might recognise and imagine someone's emotions, but whether we do something about it relies on whether we want to, and whether we are capable of it. This takes some additional maturity before the blatant self-interest of the preschooler is lost, along with the egocentric motivations of their younger years. Only then can children become more able to comfort, to share with and to help others, all of which are stages of development we need to be aware of before we expect too much from our developing little ones.

To nurture these responses it is obviously beneficial that children can see and pick up on the feelings around them, as well as have opportunities to respond. You might also want to demonstrate how you react warmly to a friend's feelings, offering support and considering the actions that are best suited. You might like to talk about how they can help a friend or people in the community, how sometimes it might be nicer to volunteer your time to help someone else rather than making a charitable donation. As you help children to recognise how they could use their own ideas, try to give them opportunities to do so if you can.

The foundations of positive social interactions

During a social encounter, children are learning to manage a number of complex processes. At times, especially if emotions are becoming involved, a child's immature brain may struggle, begin to feel uncomfortable and respond from its more primitive regions. But you can actively help them to recognise these moments and take a breath. You can teach them some strategies that help them tap back into their higher intelligence as they learn to manage their responses and actively choose their actions in ways they can rely on throughout their life.

Once children have learnt to recognise and understand, firstly their own emotions and then the emotions of others, they can then learn to respond more constructively to some possibly difficult encounters that may otherwise derail their play. When they can begin to understand the feelings that may have prompted another child's response, irrational and hurtful things said in the heat of the moment may be easier to recover from.

And as they learn to master these complex processes, valuable life lessons are being learnt.

When you support your children with this, you are developing an awareness and curiosity in them about the ways in which other people feel. Through the games you play and the books you share you can support children to recognise the behaviours on display. As you talk with them about the people and emotions they see around them, they can imagine how a given situation must feel. Through these opportunities, help children to think about the emotions that might be making a person act in a particular way and how they too could act differently.

Once you help them consider how someone else might be feeling, talk about how you could support this person as they begin to feel better. You might like to think about how all relationships need give and take from time to time as we try to understand each other's feelings and that all our actions influence and affect everyone around us.

You can also model these ideas in the ways you interact with them and the choices you make. Perhaps when you step on a brick you had asked them to tidy away, remind them that you have a choice over whether you continue with a negative emotion or actively seek to change it. By guiding children as they learn to recognise their emotions and manage them in the moment, they are better equipped to manage testing social encounters when emotions may be running high and to repair any damage that has been done after the fact.

Understanding

Understand the importance of good communication in the development of caring, two-way relationships

During their early childhood, children are continually developing ideas about how the world works and their place within it. Through every communication and social exchange, they are learning to engage and understand the people around them. They are establishing their sense of self, identifying who they are and the qualities they are looking for in a good friend, all at the same time as that potential friend is doing the same thing. This is a complex process and relationships can be tough, especially at a time when you are just learning and developing these skills for yourself. Things can be said and heard in ways that they were not meant. Feelings and emotions can run high and the behaviours they trigger are not yet well controlled. Despite this, displays of these feelings and emotions are a normal and natural part of the process that need supporting as children learn to understand, manage and effectively express them.

Supporting children through difficult processes of social connections

From the day they are born, a child is learning to understand and manage their emotions and behaviours. This is a complex process that will take years and many experiences to perfect, some of which experiences will have more successful outcomes than others. It is then so important to acknowledge a child's attempts at social interactions, recognising these interplays and the learning that is occurring, rather than being too quick to correct them. While a child may be quick to resort to less-than-perfect responses, it is important that we understand why. Their social and emotional development is not mature enough at this stage to be fully managed and continual corrections will simply dent their confidence as they practice and develop these skills.

When you see unkind behaviours, know that these are the responses of someone who has not yet learnt to manage their feelings in more socially acceptable ways. This is something that needs further teaching. This is not evidence of an "unkind child" with worrying character flaws that need changing. If you see a child being unkind, talk to them about what they are doing and the consequences, offering them alternative actions they can try. Remind them of the kind and compassionate behaviours you have modelled or that you saw in a book together as you imprint these responses in their mind. This is much more effective than reprimands that draw attention to the negative behaviours and instead, help them to see themselves as a caring, compassionate person.

Figure 6.2 Children are learning how to socially interact through every experience of it. Bringing children of different ages together naturally requires additional elements of kindness that both are learning from.

If we can place a strong value on empathy and being a caring person, children will be more motivated to respond in similar ways. Surrounded by examples of acts of kindness, gentle tones and kind words, children will emulate these behaviours which will, in time, help to form this part of their identity (Figure 6.2). You are supporting this process every time you effectively model your more difficult emotions. Every time they see you and others managing your reactions and behaviours in socially acceptable ways, they are learning how to do the same while seeing this as the automatic and expected way of responding. You can also show a child that they are not wrong in feeling negative thoughts, but when they do, that they have choices in how they respond to them. To support this, you might like to use phrases such as "I can see you're very angry right now, so please use your words and tell me why you are angry" or "I am listening, there is no need to hit or throw to get my attention, just use your words". Acknowledge every step towards a more positive response, even if in the early days this is just an extra breath before they throw the book across the room.

Understanding the child who is struggling

As you look to develop a child's social skills, it is so important that you are mindful of the deep-rooted impact of what you are doing. In these early years, you are also shaping the child's personal identity, informing their ideas of the person they are and who they are likely to become. It is then important that we talk openly about feelings and relationships, using a pace and language that is right for the situation and the children involved in it. When we do so, children become better able to understand another person's perspectives as well as understanding that the views or feelings of a friend are not that dissimilar to their own, even if they themselves may feel vastly different to the other children around them. Through these processes, children are then gain-

Figure 6.3 Bringing children together with a shared interest can help them to see that we have much in common, making differences of opinion easier to manage when they do arise.

ing a broader, less self-centred perspective – an important process in allowing deeper friendships the opportunity to grow (Figure 6.3).

As you look to support a child who is struggling to socially interact, you may find that they begin to react defensively in social situations. While you are keen for them to engage and practice their skills, they may seem keen to avoid or quick to sabotage any opportunity. But don't we all seek to avoid what makes us feel uncomfortable? Pressuring them into it will only establish a contest of wills and associate more negativity around it, making the situation worse.

As you look to nurture these skills, be patient. Allow children to go at their own pace as they take this time to develop their own character. If a child feels that they cannot be themselves around you, or in this environment, you may be storing up trouble for the future. If they fail to develop a lack of security in familiar places, they may look to attach themselves to others for support as they get older, even if that means sacrificing their own integrity. So, be sure that children always feel accepted for who they are in this moment, while offering them the support and encouragement to be all they can possibly be.

Keeping it manageable

Lastly, manage your expectations. Social skills can be difficult to work through, both physically and mentally, so take a close look at how much you are expecting of your children. Be particularly careful of the environment that children are being expected to manage these skills within and the additional expectations that are being placed on them at the time. For example, do not be surprised if you are trying to manage some regrettable behaviours and questionable responses at a time when children are tired or hungry. We can all get cranky in these moments, so ensure that children are well rested and well fed before you question their reactions with any greater level of worry.

Then, give children the time and space they need to establish these skills while they are young. Social and emotional skills are the bedrock of many of the other areas of development that are occurring. Without these being securely developed, a child is going to struggle. This is so much more important than being rushed through various different activities, no matter how exciting you think they might be. Maximising a child's ability to form friendships and develop good social skills establishes advantages within them that will stay with them for life. So, accept them for who they are, while offering them the support and encouragement to develop these deeply impactful life-long skills.

Support

Be supported in offering play opportunities designed to develop social interactions, to recognise when children are struggling and the measures you can put in place

Children are developing their skills through various styles of play from day one, from observing others, to playing alongside them, to total immersion in games that they need to help formulate rules for. All of this depends on the child's age and their stage of development. So, avoid deciding for them, and instead give them lots of rich opportunities to settle into the style of play they are ready and for and feel comfortable with.

Through these exchanges children are learning about relationships and what it takes to make and keep friends. For children of any age this can be a struggle at times and may require some gentle support and direction. However, your most important role in supporting this process is in giving children lots of opportunities to practice at it. The first thing to do when supporting a child's developing social skills is then to create opportunities for them to play with other children with the time, space and resources they need along with an understanding of their developing social skills in mind. You must then stand back and observe, without being too quick to intervene, as children are given the opportunities they need to explore these developing skills. And yes, to make mistakes as they learn from them within a safe environment.

Talking things through

When things have gone wrong and a child is reaching out to you for support, talk with them about what has happened. You can help your children through this process by talking about the social dilemmas being faced. But be careful; this can become very personal very quickly, so a better tactic is often to talk about characters in a book or game you have played. As you draw attention to the friendship issues being faced, you can help them think about the emotions they might be feeling and the actions that were taken. As you explore what happened next, you can help children to understand that this is a process that no one gets right all the time. This will help avoid feelings of criticism or result in the child becoming overwhelmed, especially with older children who can feel acutely self-conscious if their social behaviours are criticised. Remember that if this were to happen, you are only likely to see them reject any suggestion you make and shut down.

As you help connect a child with their feelings and the feelings of those around them, you can invite ponderings such as "I wonder how that would have felt" as you retain some distance and avoid triggering an immediate defence mechanism. Always be careful of assigning any blame to anyone or suggestions of labelling and instead phrase any difficult discussions with language that invites good intentions with statements such as "I'm sure you didn't mean to" or "You probably didn't realise". Not only does this avoid excuses and make it more likely that a child will hear what you have to say, but it also invites them to create this positive image of themselves.

Fostering skills of togetherness

Make the environment a place where friendships can grow by having inviting activities and opportunities for children to come together. Make these areas where children can engage freely over a common interest, but where you can also discretely observe and offer some gentle support if needed. You could set up a group task that involves a basic level of group coordination, with an incentive for its completion – for example, building a den or getting things ready for a picnic. It might not be the best lunch they have ever

Figure 6.4 Group tasks help children develop the vocabulary and social skills needed for healthy relationships.

had, but so much will be learnt from the experience of working together to make it worth the questionable decisions made along the way (Figure 6.4).

As children engage through these collaborative tasks together, they will be communicating within a place of safety. Understanding the benefits of pulling together and the satisfaction when the task is completed. You can then take this a step further by giving the children opportunities to behave in compassionate ways towards the others involved. Model responses and moments of kindness with phrases such as "Thank you, that was a big help to me" or "That was kind of you to help each other lift that, I can see it would have been too difficult to do it on your own". Through these gentle reminders, the children will be recognising the positive impact they can have on others and the benefits that interacting with a friend can bring. And if there is conflict, talk with them about a solution, showing good principles of cooperation as you listen and get everyone involved. Whether the task is ever completed or not is less important than these skills that are learnt along the way and the fun that is experienced.

Supporting sharing skills

You can support your children to develop the social skills of sharing, turn-taking and cooperation through the games that you play, such as "I went shopping and I bought…", moving through the alphabet together, supporting each other as you take turns and try to get further than you did last time. Simple board games help introduce social rules and offer opportunities to manage conflict when things don't go well, while you are in the safety of an environment they feel secure in.

If they are struggling with the skills required, you can begin with games where they are playing with an adult. In this scenario, the dynamics are less confrontational and a win all the sweeter. If they do find this difficult, talk about their feelings, their chosen behaviours and the consequences. Once any hurt feelings have calmed down, use this opportunity as you consider better strategies for next time. This also offers you an insight into why a child may be struggling around other children and the particular social skills they need further support with.

Supporting the shy child

If a child is shy, support their attempts at social interactions by demonstrating techniques yourself and by offering them a place of safety to return to. Avoid pressuring them as they have a go and practice on their own terms, which will become easier over time. No one likes to feel forced into something, especially if this is something we feel very uncomfortable doing. Instead, offer lots of opportunities for mixing in different situations and environments, especially those that offer imaginative play where children can safely develop their confidence, creativity and self-control in ways that allow for their own abilities in these areas to grow. Through these opportunities children have the safe space to explore the skills they need and to practice them on their terms.

Managing expectations

And lastly, manage your expectations, especially around any big transitions. Social skills can be difficult to work through, both physically and mentally, so take a close look at how much you have scheduled for the week and take care to prioritise and let some things go. Try to avoid any excessive additional demands, especially when a child is on the verge of a big developmental break through.

Teachable moments only come when children are not too upset to talk or listen. So, take things slowly and allow your children to master these complex skills over time as you respect the person they are becoming, treasuring the characteristics that make them who they are as you help them to grow in their own ways.

Note

1 Warneken, F., & Tomasello, M. (2006). Altruistic helping in human infants and young chimpanzees. *Science*, 311, 1301–1303.

7 Understanding young children's friendships

Research shows that when a child has close friends, with mutual shared interests, their self-esteem is likely to be higher. As they get older, these children tend to feel less lonely, they are able to demonstrate a more positive attitude towards school and they are likely to cope better in stressful situations. They are also less vulnerable to the potentially difficult behaviours of other children. When playing within a friendship group, a child also has opportunities to develop their communication skills and to learn important social skills, such as empathy and cooperation, that the other children around them are becoming more proficient in.

Figure 7.1 Friendships are so important to us, even from a young age.

We cannot make friends for our children, neither can we hasten their social and emotional development. But what we can do with a little understanding, however, is to support and encourage their ability to connect with other children and to develop the courage they need to engage. By knowing about and recognising a child's developmental stage, you can interpret their social behaviours, seeing the meaning behind them and using this as you guide their effective responses to social challenges.

As they become more familiar with the styles of play that the other children are engaging in, they will become better at entering into it. Through these experiences, they can then develop the skills of recognising and accommodating the other children's perspectives, helping them to become better able to make the deeper and more meaningful friendships of the older years and develop connections that are more likely to withstand the turbulent times of any relationship (Figure 7.1).

DOI: 10.4324/9781003327042-8

In the first chapter in this book I mentioned Maslow and his hierarchy of needs. As you will remember, this theory suggests that until a child's complex social needs are taken care of, their desire for close emotional relationships will drive their behaviour and that, without the opportunity or the means to form secure friendships, their attention on other areas will be lacking. Throughout their lives, a child needs to make connections with other people. If a child is struggling, any other experience they could be having is likely to take a back seat. It is then so important that we support children in developing these techniques while they are young and in a safe environment to do so.

Knowledge

Know the different levels of friendship children engage in as their friendships mature

Children will be going through all kinds of stages as they are growing up, learning about the world and how to function within it. At the same time as managing friendship dilemmas, their immature brains are also struggling to deal with all the physical and emotional limitations of what it means to be a young child. As a result, their expectations and desires in a situation may be unmatched to their understanding of it or the verbal skills they have to achieve their goals, alongside a potential friendship group who may well be feeling the same way. As children leave their toddler years behind, they are developing a more mature understanding of their own mind along with a greater level of independence and self-control than they experienced just a few months ago. Alongside this, the nature of their social interactions is changing, supporting new ways of playing and the maturity of the friendships that are beginning to form.

These social interactions and the wide range of friendships that are developing are very important to young children. However, their skills at forming and keeping them are, as yet, in their infancy. Much as they may play at "Being mummy" or "Being daddy", they are also playing at "Being a good friend" – a concept that is being as equally informed by the examples they have around them as all the other roles they will try on for size. But as they are playing with these ideas of what a relationship means, they will be doing so with their immature view of the world, as will the children with whom they are trying to establish these friendships with.

So, what makes a "good friend"?

For some children, friendships seem to come easy. They seem able to make new alliances with ease as they fall into play with one group at the swings before engaging in different styles of interaction in the sandpit. For other children, they seem to struggle at forming the bonds, of being included in the play going on around them or in keeping it going. So, what skills does it take to be included within a group of playing children?

As you would expect, many research studies have looked at this question. These studies are typically conducted in school playgrounds where large groups of children have the opportunity to come together and play, alongside spending time in the classroom. This dynamic allows children to get to know one another while observing the behaviour traits they tend to display. One such psychology study[1] conducted at the University of Illinois asked children "Who are the most popular children in your class?" The researchers found that the children who were considered the most popular were not necessarily those who were well liked. Popular children were likely to act friendly, but with a tendency to show more hostile tendencies, using this to increase their own social power and control within the group. Their findings went on to make several interesting observations.

- Children who do not stand out in any particular way have an average reputation for being liked

- The more aggressive children, the assertive rule breakers, tend to be well liked by some, but not by others

- Children who are less outgoing tend to be neither particularly liked nor overly disliked by their peers, but they don't seem to be lonely and tend to be well liked by adults and teachers

- Children who tend to be friendly, to be easy-going and cooperative are considered kind and are often included in the play; these children tend to be assertive when needed but are rarely disruptive

Studies suggest that similar tiers and groupings tend to be found in any group of school children, with most children settling into the middle levels where genuine friendships can be found. The children we need to be more concerned about are those that tend to become disliked by their peers. It is these children that are more likely to experience a wide range of problems. Now, before the transition to school when these new relationship-making skills will be forming, it is a good time to understand the techniques being used and be on hand to help guide them.

Stages of friendships in children

Psychologist Robert Selman[2] identified five levels, or stages, in children's friendships.

1. **Three to six years: "I want it my way"**
   Children in this stage, Selman suggests, view friendships as something in the moment. They are most likely to spend time with whichever child is nearby and sharing similar activities in the moment. While they like and often talk about the idea of having preferred friends, these are not reliable relationships and will change frequently.

2. **Five to nine years: "What's in it for me?"**
   At this stage, children understand that a friendship goes beyond an immediate activity. However, a friend is considered to be someone that has just shared their sweets

or picked them for a game. They are unlikely to think much about what they themselves are contributing to this relationship.

3. **Six to twelve years: "By the rules"**
   By this stage a child is now considering a friend's perspective in addition to their own, but not necessarily at the same time. While they are genuinely concerned with fairness and taking turns within the relationship, children at this stage will be expecting to gain favours in return.

4. **Eight to fifteen years: "Caring and sharing"**
   By now, friends are becoming increasingly important. They are helping each other to solve problems and are used to confide personal thoughts and feelings. Children now know how to compromise and will genuinely treat their friends kindly because they care about the other person, not because they want something from them in return.

5. **Aged twelve and beyond: "Mature friendship"**
   Children will now place a high value on emotional closeness with their friends. Empathy, trust and support are important and their friends remain emotionally close, even when they are separated from them. At this stage, children can accept and appreciate differences between themselves and their friends and will feel less threatened if their friends have other relationships.

As children progress through these stages of friendships there are likely to be some conflicts, which we will look at in more detail in the next chapter. But these bumps in the road are something that every child needs to experience if they are going to be able to form healthy relationships in the future.

Research looking at friendships and the effects of peer pressure show, unsurprisingly, that pre-teens are likely to be influenced by the actions and choices of the children they spend time with. Whether this is the effect of others lowering their inhibitions or that children are simply drawn to children with similar inclinations is less clear. What is better understood is that unsurprisingly, children tend to be friends with those children that they have the opportunities to spend time with, going on to develop similar interests with and similarities to them (Figure 7.2). It is then important, while our children are young, that they develop a good understanding of the person they want to be, and that they find the things they enjoy and want to be associated with before they become overly influenced by the others around them.

Without having experienced the highs and lows of relationships and having

Figure 7.2 Friendships grow through the moments we share with one another.

come to recognise these as a short-term bump in the road, there is an increased risk of children being susceptible to excessive peer pressure in the future. To be able to manage these eventualities for themselves they do then need to learn what it means to contribute to a friendship, to compromise, to emotionally connect and to recognise the mutual importance of being there for one another.

Understanding

Understand how children make friendships in the early years, the social behaviours this entails and how you can support children to respond to social challenges

As we have seen, friendships are hugely important at any age. But to a growing child who is learning about their place in the world, this is a particularly important contribution towards their level of happiness and general well-being. And if they are struggling to make friends or feel like they are not well liked, this can become a deeply distressing time for any child involved, as well as for the adults that are attempting to understand the process. So, make sure that they have opportunities to engage over a shared interest or common activity without undue interruptions or distractions.

As you look to help children connect, observe their attempts at engaging and consider how open and inviting to other children they appear to be. If you are concerned about a child that seems to be having difficulties, you might like to consider whether it is their behaviours, their activities or the opportunities they are being offered that may be contributing to this, affecting the way they are portrayed to others. If none of these areas appear to suggest a problem, you may like to look a little deeper at the social behaviours they are displaying and the support they may need you to put in place.

What it takes to make a friend

Research suggests that to form friendships at any age, you need to be aware of three key elements. These may all be tricky things to master for a young child, but they are all things you can help support and put experiences in place as you facilitate opportunities for a child to practice.

■ How open someone is to the prospect of becoming a friend

■ The similarities you may have with one another

■ The shared activities that you can bond over.

Firstly then, the child needs to be aware of whether the potential friend is open to the idea of a friendship, as they learn to ask themselves, is this person interested in becoming friends? This begins from "Hello" with eye contact, smiling warmly, speaking loudly enough to be heard and saying the other person's name. If this is something a child is struggling with, these skills can be easily role played, either with you or with dolls or props as you practice what making friends might be like for them. You can also see how this is achieved in a favourite film or story where a new friendship is formed. Can they spot the techniques that were used? Maybe a kind word or an act of kindness such as lending a pencil or saving someone a seat.

Secondly, we tend to make friends with people that we perceive to be like us. For a child this may mean other children of the same age, sex or ethnicity, as well as those who may seem to have similar interests, like having a puppy for a pet, being particularly fond of cars or even having the same shoes. Children will also bond with others that appear to have the same degree of popularity or academic ability. This is because friendship tends to be a relationship between equals; the alternative to this is the "magnet theory" where children believe they must be so wonderful or funny that everyone wants to be their friend. It is then better to help children practice finding potential friends with common ground than trying to get all children to admire them for their antics.

And thirdly, it is unsurprising that children tend to be friends with those they meet through a shared activity. These are frequently organised, adult-led activities, but unstructured time together is equally important. This allows children the freedom to choose what they want to do and with whom, creating strong connections through the more meaningful interactions that are possible. So, when you consider the activities that are available, have these early friendship-making skills in the back of your mind as you think of creating ideal opportunities for practicing them (Figure 7.3).

Figure 7.3 When you offer a range of activities and resources, children will investigate what pulls their attention, meeting other children there who are interested in exploring the same ideas and a connection can form.

Why some children struggle to make friends

Making friends is a complex business involving several interconnected processes, and children do not always take this in their stride. Research shows, however, that like most of us, children tend to revert to type, following the same behavioural patterns even when placed into new environments or groups of potential friends. This would suggest that moving a struggling child so that they can make a fresh start somewhere new will have a limited impact unless something else changes alongside geography. Instead, you are better off supporting a child by actively helping them to identify and then address any potential issues before they have a chance to negatively spiral or behaviours become character forming.

Researchers have suggested four main reasons why a child may struggle to make friends.

- They are angry

- They are withdrawn

- They are out-of-sync

- They are highly emotional

If a child frequently feels angry, they may be showing aggressive behaviours and be prone to angry outbursts. At the very least, other children tend to find these outbursts disruptive to their play and in more extreme cases, they may find them rather frightening. You can help children who are struggling in this way to better understand and cope with their more difficult emotions. As they learn to manage these behaviours and outbursts they can learn to avoid repeated conflicts before it is them that is being avoided.

If a child is feeling withdrawn, they may distance themselves from others. These children may not notice or respond to friendly gestures or may themselves appear anxious or unapproachable. You can support these children by practicing social encounters within safer, more protected environments. As you model techniques they can try and offer them the guidance they need, these children can learn to become more competent and confident in social situations.

Being out-of-sync means having interests or habits that are different to their peers, perhaps appearing babyish or more mature than their years. While it may seem like a child has quite different areas of interests to many of their peers, you can help them to find something that they can have a genuine bond through even if this is quite different to the other children in the group.

If a child is highly emotional, they may be prone to crying or seeking adult attention. During these times they spend less time playing, learning, talking and interacting with the other children who again find these behaviours disconcerting and will find their friendships elsewhere. You may find it helpful to talk to these children about the consequences of these actions in language they can understand. Together, you can work through alternative behaviours when they slip into these familiar behaviour patterns. You may like to suggest that you cannot understand them if they do not use their words and avoid giving in to these tactics when they use them to gain your attention.

It is then important to observe children together as you look to recognise their natural tendencies. You are then in an informed position that will help you to support the child as they modify their more extreme behaviours and look instead for situations that work with rather than against them. For example, if a child tends to be highly physical, sports may help. If they are withdrawing through shyness, then music or theatre might be a better fit. And if they are not finding the process easy or natural, with this understanding you can then work with them to develop more targeted skills of friendship formation.

Support

Be supported to recognise potential problems as children experience making, keeping, or falling out with friends and the processes you can put in place to support this

The making, breaking, forming and reshaping of friendships and social alliances can be difficult to manage and witness for all concerned. When things get really emotive it can be tempting to wade in and want to support the children and the immature responses involved. However, research involving young children suggests that they can have just under three conflicts an hour, with friends experiencing more conflicts than non-friends simply because of the longer amounts of time they will be spending together. While children are young these conflicts tend to be less intense and quicker to resolve than our more mature relationships. But to the inexperienced friend-maker this can be a tricky thing to understand – and that is after you have made the friend in the first place. So, let us start there, with helping children to make friends in the first place.

Making contact

If a child is struggling to get involved in other children's play, observe them in an open environment where you can watch them around other children and see what happens. Within a free-play environment, children will tend to firstly watch others playing, then slide into the action without interrupting. But this can be a difficult thing to achieve when you consider the social dynamics at play and the things that can and do frequently go wrong. The easiest way for a child to become included in the play of another is when they look to join an individual child, or alternatively, a group of four or more. This way they are less likely to draw attention to themselves or overly interrupt the play. This sounds simple, but if a child is shy, lacking confidence or experience, this can go wrong for several reasons.

- They may hang back for too long

- They could stop the flow of the play

- Their attempts or suggestions are not in keeping with the play that is already underway

Watch a child who is struggling as they have a go and see if you can identify where things could go smoother. If they are too shy to try for themselves, have them observe other children and tell you what they are seeing. Did the child stand close to where the children were playing, did they retrieve a thrown ball and jump straight in, did they run into a game of tag or offer ideas for where the play could go? Once you have developed this understanding together, give them lots of opportunities to practice.

Building confidence

Even the most well-liked children are rejected about one out of every four times they try to join into existing play. So, help a struggling child to understand this and not be put off by it. If they can accept that this is going to happen, with you available to talk through any apprehension when it does, you can avoid this denting what may already be a fragile level of confidence. In these moments, help the child to simply walk away and try joining a different group or try again a few minutes later. It may also be benefi-cial to hang back and watch these processes in action with other children as they see this is a reality experienced by everyone.

Developing the skills to communicate

To make new friends, children also need the confidence and ability to talk to other children; to go up to another child and say something, possibly intro-ducing themselves, but more likely to jump straight into the play; to listen to the conversations already going on, to know whether their contribution is likely to be accepted; and to think of something appropriate to say, spotting the time and opportunity to say it and the possible consequences if their con-

Figure 7.4 Sometimes making the first move can be tough. Having a "go-between" can then help smooth this process – even when the "mid-dle-man" is a worm!

tribution is not quite on the mark. These are all skills that need to be developed and practiced. You can help your children with this through role play, observation and reflection (Figure 7.4).

Regulating difficult impulses in social situations

The behaviours and emotions that surround our children, in every environment they find themselves in, will have a big impact on their emotional development and resulting social behaviours. As they then use these influences within their social encounters, they will undoubtedly affect their peer relationships. Whether they have been surrounded with strict control or warmth and openness, a lack of affection or frequent times of emotional sharing, as children learn to make their own relation-ships they need to understand the responses they may be falling into and learn to regulate them.

Talking openly with children about this helps as you look to be sympathetic to their feelings, but constructive in helping them to see the potential consequences of their actions. Help them to see that we can all experience bad moods and have a feeling we find difficult to manage, but that we also need to find ways of regulating the behaviours these moods may trigger within us – especially around other people.

The drama of a 'best friend'

Unless you limit children to shallow relationships, close relationships with a "best" friend may form. Sometimes, however, this can be a rocky road, full of the dramas of drifting apart, being replaced or the heartache of an angry conflict. But don't avoid this; close friends are an important and deeply meaningful part of life, so rather than fearing any potential break up, help children to form multiple friendships. Encourage different types of friends, some close, others more casual, and those that are formed through different activities and interests. In this way, when they encounter difficult times or conflicts, they are more likely to be able to weather the ups and downs. While this will be distressing in the moment, it can also give children an opportunity to focus on deepening their other relationships rather than feeling all alone.

When it all goes wrong

Conflicts between young children tend to be very short, typically fewer than ten back-and-forth exchanges, with most resolved within four exchanges. In the early years these will tend to be about who has the coveted toy. A little older and squabbles tend to develop around social behaviours, things said or done or not said and done. By the teen years, arguments are mostly about relationship issues as they tend to become more elaborate and last longer, with hurt feelings that can go on for days or even months.

Usually, when it comes to conflict, boys are more likely to react with aggression to get their own way or get even, whereas girls typically seek to solve the problem. However, when it comes to relationships, the gloves are off! Girls are equally likely to endorse revenge and aggression and will interpret breaches in friendship much more harshly than the boys, tending to set a far higher level of expectations from their friends. A crucial part of any friendship is then inevitable conflict and the stages of resolution this requires and this is where we will go in the next chapter.

Notes

1 Parkhurst, J. T., & Hopmeyer, A. (1998). Sociometric popularity and peer-perceived popularity: Two distinct dimensions of peer status. The Journal of early adolescence. [Online] 18(2), 125–144.
2 Selman, R. L. (1981). The child as friendship philosopher. In S. R. Asher, & J. M. Gottman (Eds.), The Development of Children's Friendships (pp. 242–272). Cambridge: Cambridge University Press.

8 Understanding the conflicts of young children

Children go through all kinds of stages as they are growing up learning about the world and how to function within it. But now that their friendships and interactions are becoming a more important part of their day, the rules governing friendships have become a big part of this learning journey. Social and emotional development are then an important part of a child's development, as much as any other form of learning. They need to understand what their feelings are telling them, how best to react to them, how to engage with others, how to follow agreed-upon rules and routines and how to manage the inevitable conflicts. They also need to understand when others are experiencing negative emotions, how to interact during the experience and how to continue with the relationship after the fallout. This is a complex set of skills that you can guide and support children through. How you go about teaching them to understand and effectively manage their behaviours is something explored within the Secure Child chapters throughout this series of books. In *Nurturing Babies*, these are Chapters 5 and 6; in *Nurturing Toddlers*, Chapters 4 and 5; in this book, *Nurturing Children through Preschool and Reception*, Chapters 3, 4 and 5; and in the final book, *Nurturing through the Primary Years*, they are Chapters 3 and 4.

Whether you realise it or not, children begin learning about how to deal with conflicts and any associated social and emotional issues from the day they are born, with all the familiar adults in their life becoming instrumental within this process, although not necessarily in the ways that they may choose. How these adults were responded to during their own childhood phases of difficult behaviours will now be informing the ways they are predisposed to react to the children around them, who may themselves now be finding themselves surrounded by others experiencing a phase of difficult behaviours. And don't get me wrong, we can all have our moments!

Alongside this, throughout their childhood, children have been watching, seeing how different people react to different situations. And they are closely observing the behaviours that are being modelled. Now, as children are becoming more social, it is so important that we teach them the responses we would like them to learn – lessons about

DOI: 10.4324/9781003327042-9

how to process their emotions effectively, how to resolve interpersonal conflict and how to manage different kinds of social interactions, especially where there has been disagreement or a lack of communication. And maybe learn some tricks along the way!

Knowledge

Know what conflict can mean to young children and what your expectations in the moment should be

As we have explored in the last few chapters, friendships are a very important part of every child's development and sense of belonging. Unfortunately, where there are friendships, there will inevitably be a measure of conflict. If you try to think of conflicts when they arise as an inevitable part of social life, they are no longer something to be feared or avoided. Often they are simply a difference of opinion, a defence mechanism to a perceived hurt feeling or a problem that needs to be solved. Viewed in this way, you can help your children learn to identify what is at the root of the problem, to name it and to work out how to move from conflict to solution (Figure 8.1).

Figure 8.1 Conflicts are a part of the friendship process and shouldn't be feared or avoided. However, they may need a little help in these early days.

It may also help to realise that research looking at the behaviours of preschoolers has noted about one-fifth of the conflicts children enter into are resolved immediately with the children continuing to play together soon afterwards, especially if one of the children gave an apology, a hug or offers to share. However, as children are getting a little older, their friendships are progressing through the more mature definitions outlined in the previous chapter. Relationships are then beginning to take on quite a different meaning, emotions may be more deeply hurt and others may be drawn into the mix.

Being able to engage with others

The ability to work with others is a staple of any school classroom – and job application, for that matter. It is an important life skill and one that every child will be learning about from their early years. Being able to come together and share our expertise and ideas gives rise to tremendous insight and levels of understanding that would otherwise not be possible. But this also places a child in a position of comparison. What can they do compared to those around them and what do other people think of them when they do it? Their responses will be based on the different set of experiences, opinions and outlooks a child approaches a situation with, and their expectations will be fuelled through every experience that precedes it (Figure 8.2). Now imagine you are a young child struggling to voice or express this opinion or a teenager seeing your own opinion as the one true way forward, and we can see how conflicts arise.

Such collaborations are then not always easy and some children seem to be better at it than others. But now

Figure 8.2 Within any group activity we can become focused on intended learning objectives, however there is so much more learning going on.

they are getting older and their styles of play and engagement are maturing, children will be coming together with more regularity. This will inevitably result in more conflict but being together is a social skill and as such can be taught and developed with practice.

What conflict means to a child

The magnitude of any problem often lies within a child's perception of it. And if this involves a mean comment or action from the person they feel is the most important person in the world to them – well, at least for today – a child's conflicts can feel all encompassing. However, if you seek to rescue children from their problems, they will not learn to manage them for themselves next time or to develop the belief in themselves that they can. But to learn from these moments, they firstly need to be in a state where they can hear you, when the less emotional areas of their brain are no longer calling the shots and when constructive memories can be established, ready for the next encounter.

When conflicts happen, it is important that we help children to see them as a natural part of life, rather than proof that everything is going wrong for them in a world that is supposed to be perfect. Help them to see conflict as a problem that needs to be solved; an opportunity, rather than something to hide from or deny. When children experience solving their own problems, they are less likely to avoid taking the risks that might result in great failure or great success. They are less likely to give up when they experience setbacks and defeats and are more open to learning from adversity, using that knowledge to create new opportunities.

Creating a nurturing environment for friendships

As children get older, you can talk with them about the friendships that are important to them and how they think these can be developed. You can help them think about the importance of rules and ask for their thoughts on what they should be as you talk about letting others speak without interrupting, sharing nicely and being kind. You may like to help children to think about the different behaviours they see on display, without naming names, as they think about what they are doing and the consequences this may result in.

When we invite children to talk about their behaviours and the emotions that have triggered them, it no longer becomes a feared area that needs to be avoided. Instead, it is viewed as a natural part of the social world we live in. As they become more experienced in talking about their feelings and their expectations of others, you can invite children to describe what friendship means. You can talk specifically about their actions and those of others. You can ask them why it is important to act in certain ways and what they think the consequences of certain actions, positive and negative, might be.

And practice really listening without interrupting. Focus on hearing what the child is saying without any personal intention, opinions or views, looking out for any feelings they may be mentioning. You can then reflect your understanding back to the child, even if they have not been able to use names for their feelings. When you label these emotions, you are validating them for the child and helping them to identify them in the future. You are also showing them that you are really listening and that their feelings are important. Within this environment, a child can feel recognised, valued and esteemed. They learn that they can communicate openly with you as you show them the importance of responsibility and honesty. And they will develop a sense of who they are in the world, ready for when they go out into it.

The development of the "clique"

As children progress through these stages, they may also experience social cliques. These tend to be friendship groups of about three to nine children who are drawn together, often through a similar activity, attitudes or interests, and they may establish certain "rules" within the clique and recognisable behaviours may form. While this exclusivity may seem to be a negative influence, cliques are a natural progression within intimate friendships. By the time children reach their teen years, these cliques will tend to merge. This is seen as individual, more intimate relationships become more important to the child than seeking to conform and fit into a group. But for now, and in the years to come, they will tend to attract some drama.

Whether your children are become affected by this new development, whether their actions are being affected by them or if they are worried about not being accepted into one, responding in a caring way is key as you offer some perspective and help them maintain a balanced outlook on what is going on. This may involve some conflict and this can be painful for all concerned, including those looking on from the sidelines. It is then important that you avoid getting caught up in it and maintain that distance and perspective that a struggling child may need as you direct their attention back to the importance of real friendship and leave pursuits of popularity, status or approval alone.

Understanding

Understand how to use this inevitable conflict as a learning exercise and what the adult role needs to be within it

The process of making and keeping friends may well come with great frustrations, for everyone involved. However, being on the receiving end of strong emotions from those they are looking to for love, support and guidance can have long-term effects on a child's dignity and self-worth. Children are in the process of understanding their emotions and learning to manage them. This takes time and they will make mistakes. But if you want them to grow up with understanding and respect, for themselves and others, you need to show them respect and understanding. If you want them to have a voice, to be able to express their own needs and ask for what they want, their needs must be respected and listened to. Even when these are being communicated in difficult ways.

From an early age, children are learning that aggressive responses tend only to lead to further aggression, even when these are painful lessons to be learnt. If you want to help children avoid potentially escalating the issues they find themselves facing without the maturity to do it well, they need your guidance (Figure 8.3). Similarly, if they are seen as too passive this may be perceived as a sign of weakness and may simply invite further aggression just as effectively. Assertive and non-violent methods of conflict resolution, on the other hand, establish mature and courageous responses. And these are all things we can help our children with.

The conflicts we learn from

Children are learning from every experience they are having. When it comes to conflict, they need to learn constructive, responsible and non-violent ways to manage strong emotions as they arise. The trouble is that conflicts are often faced when emotions are running high. Children will then tend to swing into learnt behaviours and responses before the thinking part of their brain has a chance to engage, so it is hugely important that they are surrounded by calm and effective demonstrations of conflict resolution, even before they understand the messages this is imprinting into their developing brain.

As difficult as it may be at times, strive to demonstrate conflict as a time to negotiate and cooperate, rather than a battle that needs to be won. Be open to talking about problems and conflicts in the home or setting, sharing the steps

Figure 8.3 Sometimes all that is needed is a knowledgeable adult and a timely moment of calm.

you have taken to solve an issue. If children learn to see this as an opportunity for people to talk and listen to each other, it can become an opportunity to develop assertive negotiation skills. As they learn from the feelings, ideas and wishes of all involved, including their own, they can develop the transferable skills they need, ready to resolve their own conflicts. Offer them the skills they need to solve many of their own problems without you, even when they do not initially realise that they can. These are skills that will transfer into school, the workplace and the street.

When genuine difficulties are encountered, they are often wrapped up in a multitude of problems. But when we can introduce our children to problem-solving processes, they can learn to think their way through their problems, resolving them for themselves. We can do this by firstly teaching them to break the issue into solvable elements that they can control, understanding who owns each element and accepting what cannot be changed. Then give them the autonomy to act. Through these processes they are learning that no problem is so great that it cannot be solved and, whilst at times they may need advice and guidance, to have faith and belief in themselves that will see this conflict resolved.

Help them understand their strong emotions

Children do not have a well-established sense of time. When huge emotions overwhelm them, they can feel like this will be with them forever, good or bad. And when things go wrong, they cannot imagine a time in the future when they won't feel this bad. That is why it can be heartbreaking when a trip to the park comes to an end. While these passionate feelings are a trait to be savoured, any unregulated feelings may well intensify and strong emotions need to be regulated.

If a favoured toy gets broken or plans change, a four- or five-year-old may be distraught with grief. If they detect an element of injustice, they may be furious. While it can be difficult to talk to a furious five-year-old, this is exactly the time when they are feeling the emotions you want them to learn about. If emotions begin to run high, remember, this is about simply stating facts; there is no need for emotion or debate, you don't need to get angry, to nag, warn or in time even comment as a look will do. Simply know the strategies you can employ and walk calmly through them as you remind yourself and the child that these extreme feelings will pass, that they are able to take control and that you are here to help them do it.

Children need opportunities to try

As you give your children opportunities to solve their own conflicts, avoid being too quick to rush in. Instead, stand back, listen and see what happens. And, if this does then require intervention, look to them for a plan. Younger children may need a few options but wait to see what solutions they offer. This may be to cooperate, although this is unlikely. It may be to avoid, as both children move to something new. Or they may come up with a plan that everyone can agree to. Discourage any suggestions of retaliation, no matter how tempting they may find this to be, and use these suggestions to warn them that this is only likely to make matters worse. When everyone is calm enough to think things through, talk through the issue that arose and try to understand the behaviours that were triggered by considering the possible feelings that were prompting them.

Use the opportunity to foster cooperation

You can foster cooperation by giving children cooperative tasks. They do not have to be complicated or long lasting but should involve at least a basic level of group coordination and cooperation as the children learn to negotiate the strategies they can use. Plan a performance for this afternoon, build a den using only household objects, even structure the tallest tower out of marshmallow and dried spaghetti! If there is conflict, have them talk through a solution. Encourage direct discussion of the methods, maybe draw up a plan beforehand as you observe and scaffold their cooperation and methods of compromise, ensuring everyone has their turn to listen and be heard.

Teach your children to listen to all sides of the story, to use their heads and then their mouths and to come up with a plan that everyone can agree to as they learn life skills for handling problems and conflicts on a grander scale. After all, you often cannot control what happens to you, but you can control what it is doing to you. And as you are helping children to manage their conflicts, acknowledge what their problems must feel like. But tell them that you know they can handle it whilst giving them the message that you are there to guide and support if they need you. However, if they are regularly finding themselves in an argument, fixated on always being right, help them understand that explaining, listening and compromising will get more positive responses from their friends than simply insisting. It is after all better to lose the occasional argument than to lose a friend.

Support

Be supported in implementing a plan for conflict resolution that empowers children in ways that they can learn from in the future

Through applying constructive and consistent techniques, you can teach your children how to respond with assertive, rather than aggressive or passive actions. As they learn to express their feelings clearly, they can learn to say no in situations where they may feel pressured or uncomfortable. Familiar with the experience of standing up for themselves, they are gaining the skills to respond verbally without fighting and to walk away from more dangerous situations. And in doing so, they show themselves as confident and resourceful and tend to be the last target for destructive behaviours from others.

These skills begin early on and are supported every time you interact with your children, especially as they are getting older and taking greater ownership of their behaviours and actions. When you engage with your children, you can ask them to honestly consider the things that have happened and the possible resolutions available to them, and you can establish a set of techniques that they can follow. As these skills become more familiar over time, they will become better able to solve their own conflicts independently, empowering children in ways that can prevent difficulties from escalating and can teach them valuable skills for life.

Calm it down

Often, when a conflict has occurred, emotions can be running high. The first thing you need to do then, once you have dealt with any spilling blood, is to give the children time to calm down. You are unlikely to achieve anything like a successful negotiation or a meaningful resolution when a situation is emotionally fraught. So, if the conflict has spiralled into a heated argument, give all parties the opportunity, understanding and space they need as you encourage both sides to take a moment. As you give the children this opportunity to tell their side of what happened, be sure to actively listen and validate the feelings they are expressing. Remember, their feelings are neither good nor bad; it is the resulting behaviours that you are looking to address.

As you ensure that all those directly involved have had a chance to voice their opinion, be sure that they are also listening to and hearing the opinions of others. At the same time, remain calm yourself. This may be enough to solve the problem, in which case make it clear that you knew they could handle it and let the play continue. If not, as soon as they are able to listen and hear, offer three potential options for them to choose to follow next. When you offer a child two options, they will be quick to spot the one they think you want them to choose and will simply go for the alternative. When you give them three options it makes them pause and think, which is often enough to calm themselves in the process. For example, you might like to say "I can see you are upset, you need to calm down and then decide.

- You can go to the other room

- You can sit on the bench, or

- You can sit on my lap".

Acknowledge the feelings that fuelled it

Once the children have managed to calm themselves down enough to communicate, support them as they talk to each other about the feelings that led to the altercation. You can support this by encouraging them to use phrases that own their feelings, "When I heard you say… I felt…" rather than "When you said this … you made me feel".

You can then acknowledge and validate their feelings as you repeat what they have said back to them, whilst using the opportunity to illustrate the unfortunate choice they made with regards to their actions: "I can see that you are angry, it is okay to be angry, but it is not okay to hit". You can then ask them, "What can you do to help the other child (the situation) to feel (to get) better?" In this way you are moving the focus of all this negative emotion away from attaching blame. At the same time, you are helping children to recognise and name their feelings, both by acknowledging their own and the other child's. If the children valued the relationship before the conflict, help them to keep this in mind. It may just take time for tempers to cool, or a kind gesture or shared activity they can work at together.

When offering children effective methods of conflict resolution, remember to consider their age. A study at Florida Atlantic University[1] suggested that children between two and ten years old are most likely to resolve peer conflicts by forcing one child to back down. From 11 to 18 years they are more likely to walk away, leaving issues unresolved rather than risking the friendship. It is not until our early 20s that we negotiate our way to conflict resolution. So, while you may have sleepless nights worrying about today's upset and the ways in which you handled it, it is important to keep it in perspective. Children's feelings and relationships change rapidly and they are likely to have already dismissed the whole event. If not and the negative feelings are rumbling on, it is time to formulate a plan (Figure 8.4).

Formulate a plan

- **Identify and define the conflict**
  Begin by helping children to use their words as they state what is going wrong. Focus on feelings rather than actions at this stage as you demonstrate and use your more-developed empathy to support this process and potentially diffuse much of the anger.

- **Break the issue down into individual problems**
  Look to understand what has caused the dispute, and then, what has caused that problem as you keep digging a little deeper towards the root of the problem. Keep going through this process until you are left with distinct issues, some of which they can control. Then help them to accept the things that they are not in control of and recognise those they have the power to change.

- **List potential options for solving the conflict**
  Any considered solution a child suggests is more likely to work than anything you propose, as they will be more invested in having their own solutions work. So, talk openly about

Figure 8.4 Disagreements, mistakes and misunderstandings will come and go. Friendships can last a lifetime.

each suggestion as you consider the action proposed and its likely consequence, both in the short term and in the long term.

■ **Choose the action to take and make a plan together**
Whilst these plans may not work every time, the scene is now set for a frank discussion, centred on feelings that, again, come without blame. As you talk together about the potential actions that could be taken, think about the associated consequences, both the positive and the negative as you are improving the chances of these plans working next time.

■ **Consider how the problem could be avoided in the future**
Frank conversations here may see you supporting children as they learn the skills of being able to let some things go – something we could all perhaps do with a little support in from time to time. While we all need our voice to be heard, there are times when it is better not to respond or to move on from the situation. Help your children to consider whether this is one of those times.

■ If it only happened once, is it likely to happen again? If not, let it go

■ Was it deliberate? If not, let it go

■ Did it happen days ago? If so, definitely let it go.

Note

1 Laursen, B., and G. Pursell. (2011). Conflict in peer relationships. In K. H. Rubin, W. M. Bukowski, & B. Laursen (Eds.), Handbook of Peer Interactions, Relationships, and Groups (pp. 267–286). New York: Guilford Press, 93.

9 Preparing for school

As we have considered throughout this set of books, during the years prior to starting school, children undergo a fantastic transformation from the baby they were just a few years ago. As well as dramatic physical growth, they have formed more than two hundred trillion brain cell connections or synapses, mapping out the structure and workings of their developing brain. Forming around 80 per cent of their basic brain architecture, these social and emotional structures are now established for life. Dependent on every experience and opportunity that they have been afforded, they are now ready to respond to the extremely personal evolving experiences still to come.

As highly motivated learners, a child's capacity for active and independent thought has been limitless as they have embraced every opportunity, learning so much in such a short time. But the landscape of learning is about to change. Their continuing desire for experimentation, for trial and error, personal choice and social engagements is about to be confined somewhat within a school classroom where an internal desire for personal, contextual and physically embraced learning may become streamlined into lesson objectives, timetables and possibly a designated place to sit still.

As many can find themselves disengaging from learning following this transition, it is important that we embed the effective characteristics of lifelong learners in our children, embracing this foundational stage and resisting any urges to propel them into more mature methods too soon, recognising that here and now we are laying the foundations of all their future learning, ready for them to take into any new environment. To do otherwise can derail the learning experience as children begin to question why their natural instincts for learning are being restricted or why school-based approaches of learning are simply not for them. It's a feeling you may yourself be familiar with, despite great personal achievements later in life.

As we look at ways of securing the most auspicious beginnings for all children it is important that we remember the incredible growth and development that is occurring during this highly sensitive period. Having established a positive relationship with a

DOI: 10.4324/9781003327042-10

child, the attachment you have with them can be used to encourage open conversations as you help them to retain the belief they have in themselves, their motivations and, by extension, their future behaviours in the classroom. All of these are essential to their mental and physical health, as well as their future learning and educational attainment.

Knowledge

Know the abilities children need to develop now if they are to manage well in the school classroom and how these are so much more important at this stage than knowing letters and numbers

As you will be well aware, every moment of a young child's early years is steeped in critical moments of growth and development. This highly sensitive period is felt throughout their mind and body, but also in the person they are becoming, their attitudes towards learning and their perceptions of it. This is precious time that no degree of future interventions can make up for (Figure 9.1).

Figure 9.1 The lessons being learnt in the early years will stay with a child for the rest of their lives… all of them.

However, in these last years before children transition into formal education, they may be experiencing a great many conflicting emotions. With their reactions feeding off the enthusiasm and trepidation felt all around them, this is an important time to consider the messages we convey as we look at supporting the developing and changing needs of our children in these vital years before school.

- The attachments they are making are informing every future relationship

- The language surrounding them is fine-tuning their ability to hear the speech patterns required to talk, engage and voice an opinion

- Every stimulation of their body and mind is developing them physically, mentally and emotionally

- Everything from a bone in the leg to muscles in the eye and hormone receptors in the brain are adapting

- All of which is coming from every experience they are being offered

As the roots of these core processes are being laid down, they are being supported and underpinned by the more executive functions. These include flexible thinking, working memory and self-control. These abilities will, in time, help children to become better able to manage when plans change and their thinking needs to adapt. This will allow them to hold a thought in their head long enough to act on it and offer a more mature level of inhibition as they develop the ability to control their more impulsive responses.

All of these executive functions are important for children to manage once in the school classroom, for example, when plans or expectations change or if something unexpected is asked of them or if you would like for them to be able to do as they are asked, even when this involves a series of steps such as getting their workbook from their drawer and a pencil from the pot, then sitting on the carpet – and to manage all of this without lashing out at a friend who happened to get in their way. These skills have been taking root throughout their early years but as children approach the school years, they are taking on an additional level of significance.

Important now and in the years to come, executive functions support a child's skill set and are seen in their growing abilities to problem solve, to reason and to plan ahead. They allow children to self-regulate, to remain flexible as a situation fluctuates and supports their ability to control their impulses. When you consider the importance of these crucial abilities within the school environment, their need is abundantly clear. So how and where is all this brain development occurring and what can you do to support it?

Value children's deeper levels of thinking as you help them to do the same

The school classroom, by its very nature, will introduce children to formal, decontextualised learning, especially as children move up through the primary years. But, if you consider how we have evolved, our brains are not designed for demonstrated displays of knowledge. We have evolved to learn what we need when we need it and to get things done quickly in situations that matter. This is something worksheets and tests cannot offer, nor can they give a child the opportunity to show what they can really do. So now, while they have opportunity to embrace this natural way of learning, let them experience it in its full.

As we explored in previous chapters, every child will view the world in their own unique and highly personal way. Unfortunately, within the classroom, a busy teacher managing a class of 30 unique children may only be looking for the expected response to a question or request. In this environment, where all too often only one answer is sought and positively responded to, the deep-level thinking that is being displayed may be unintentionally bypassed, especially if this is not what the teacher was expecting.

Before a child finds themselves in this environment, help them to recognise the value and possibilities of their deeper levels of thinking and the opinions they voice. When they say something unexpected, explore it as you look to understand why they are thinking in that way while you have the personal knowledge and opportunities to do so. As you facilitate the full scope of their ideas you are giving their thinking the respect that comes from your interest and recognition and you are showing them that it is worthy of development and persisting with.

Value children's emotional development

In these years before school, children's personalities and social behaviour traits are also developing. They are becoming more sensitive to the interactions around them, the inspiration they are offered and the support they receive. This is influencing how they are developing in confidence, as well as higher intellectual, behavioural and social skills, all of which will impact a successful school transition far more than any academic concerns and must continue to be the focus.

Their emotional engagement is also deeply important within these learning experiences. Adverse stresses such as pressures to conform or to do well will risk an imposed sense of failure. So, be aware of what you and other influential characters are saying to them, especially on the lead-up to what will be a big change in their young life, as well as your reactions to them as they approach this significant transition.

Gaining a greater understanding of who they are

As their personalities and abilities are growing, you will be aware that the support and nurturing your children need from you is changing. They are developing a greater sense of who they are; separate from others and capable of making and experiencing their own decisions. Their growing abilities need to be embraced during this time with greater opportunities for independence and autonomy. When you can offer this to children you are extending their understanding of themselves in ways that will translate into their learning. You can do this by helping children to experience what it means to learn, to discover and understand. The more a child experiences the power of what they can discover and learn for themselves, the more they are likely to want to, gaining a positive and easily accepted view of themselves as a capable and enthusiastic learner. And this of course comes from giving children a degree of autonomy within the process (Figure 9.2).

Figure 9.2 Children are not just learning; they are learning what it means to learn and who they themselves are as a learner.

A child will also be noticing and displaying gender differences within their learning styles at this time. Girls tend to show higher attainments in areas involving co-operation, conformity, peer sociability and confidence. Perhaps because of these well-developed traits they tend to grasp pre-reading and early number concepts more easily than boys, whereas boys tend to do better with visuospatial tasks and gross-motor skills, especially those involving strength and endurance. This would suggest that the gender differences found in school results tables have already begun. So, be particularly mindful when supporting and sustaining children's developments in these areas as both will struggle in their own ways.

Understanding

Understand the impact of effective early experiences on children and the negative consequences when these have been misplaced

Historically, children have attended whatever school was closest to their homes. But that has been changing in recent years as some large school districts and school systems in large cities are increasingly allowing parents to choose where their children will go to school. Parents may then be offered numerous different options, including different types of preschools and elementary or primary placements. This process of enrolment does then have the benefit of making schools and preschool settings more diverse, along with providing motivation for parents to look around and for community leaders to make all schools and settings better, not just those located in certain neighbourhoods.

With school funding tied to the number of students who enrol, it also incentivises a school to strive for a parent's custom. So, when looking at the potential school choices on offer, we should all be mindful of what the experiences within it offer to a child. Whether this is your own child you are looking to place, or advice you are offering to parents, you should be aware of the experiences a child is likely to have and the approaches to learning that are embraced, all of which may be somewhat different to your own memories of the school classroom.

The environments we are preparing children for

The image that may spring to mind when we think of the traditional school classroom and the approaches to learning it tended to embrace was designed around the time of the Industrial Revolution. You can then be forgiven for thinking that this bears a closer resemblance to industrial manufacturing that it does with anything advocated by developmental researchers. Within this model, children were viewed much like any other product to be manufactured as those designing and leading it looked to the most efficient way of creating the desired, yet uniform product.

Within this model, requirements are predetermined and specified through desired facts and skills as detailed within an established curriculum, not dissimilar to the sizes and measurements given to a manufacturing plant. These are then used to plan lessons, which are presented according to a certain schedule, like calibrating the machines. And at the end of the process, tests were administered to assess the quality of the "product", with children passing or failing their Quality Assessment Checks, only we call them exams and qualifications. While this may work well in manufacturing, it does little to support the limitless capabilities and potential of children. Despite this, it would seem like the format in many school classrooms has changed little over the last hundred years, especially as you move up through the years.

Any attempt at systematically down-loading knowledge into the minds of a developing child is counterproductive. Children are engaging in a complex process of actively seeking to make sense of their world. They are looking to assimilate and learn from the experiences they are given, questioning their understanding and adding to their growing knowledge base. This requires exploration as they play with different ideas, and unexpected answers should be valued as teachable moments rather than mistakes to be corrected and moved on from (Figure 9.3).

Figure 9.3 Learning is a complex process that is done best when children can make the connections they need and are supplied with lots of authentic experiences, as and when they need them.

When whole-class teaching is the most common experience, many will find the pace too fast or too slow, becoming quickly distracted as they disengage from work that is either too easy or hard. While learning does happen, it is not efficient and for many is actually detrimental in the long term.

In today's climate of choice and the variety of potential approaches to learning on offer, it is vital that we are selective on behalf of the children that we care about. Informed by decades of research, we need to become mindful of the different environments and teaching styles that are embraced and be discerning on behalf of the children we are looking to support in this process. The last thing we want to do is be adapting our approaches within the play-rich early years in a misguided attempt to prepare our children for an outdated world.

The importance of good beginnings

When children arrive at school ready to take full advantage of all the experiences they are being offered, they tend to show improved levels of motivation and a lower sense of trepidation or self-doubt. This is reflected in school profiles four to six months ahead of their peers and these effects are not fleeting. Remaining throughout their first years, expectations in reading and maths are exceeded, which in turn enhances their intellectual development across the board as concepts are more easily accessed and understood.

However, children starting school demonstrating low cognitive skills are six times more likely to still be doing so a year later, with those behind at age five much more likely to be behind their peers at age seven. Without these quality foundations, children will tend to struggle with their social and emotional development too. This affects not only their academic achievements, but also their happiness, well-being, health and resilience. Schools are unable to effectively close this gap. And when children arrive at school demonstrating abilities that would suggest they are in the bottom range, they tend to stay there.

The strength of a child's abilities in the school classroom are embedded through every one of their early childhood experiences. But these need to be steeped in rich vocabulary, practical activities and social play. The influence of this could not be more pronounced. It is so important that we do all we can to nurture all our children's foundations during our time with them in the early years and to support families as they look to do the same.

Continuing the preparations that have been underway for years

However, with the start of school looming on the horizon, thoughts can still naturally turn to the need for academic preparation, possibly in the concerns of parents or the expectations felt around you. But while introducing children to letters and numbers in a variety of ways has been great all the time children have been interested in doing these things, this certainly should not be the focus of your attentions. And concerns regarding the discrete skills and abilities that they have mastered or the goals they have yet to reach should be handled with care.

And yet, the claims are constant: Children beginning formal schooling on strong foundations progress with favourable trajectories, resulting in repercussions that are felt for years to come[1]. And undoubtedly, this is true, as many product manufacturers will tell you. But there is no programme or magic product you can buy. And there is no set of worksheets to follow in the final months of preschool that will ever adequately prepare a child for all they are about to face. Indeed, considering "school readiness" in the months prior to starting school is, in many ways, years too late.

The process of preparing a child for school and indeed a lifetime of learning has been going on for a long time. It began even before they were born and has been embedded within every experience both you and their families have offered to them since birth. This will now continue as they progress through these lead-up years as you embrace the unique features, freedoms and possibilities they bring. So, avoid rushing into the constraints of lesson plans and predetermined goals that will all too soon be upon them.

Support

Be supported in offering rich experiences, rather than ticked-off goals, allowing children to remain engaged and motivated learners

It is so important that we offer our children every opportunity to develop the skills and abilities that will make all the difference to them in the years to come. But thinking solely of preparing them for starting school is vastly underestimating the importance of their early years and the potential that every child has inside them. Instead of looking towards "school readiness" I would then urge you to consider what it means to a child to learn. Rather than preparing them for the school classroom, think about how it feels to walk into the school for the first time and the deep-rooted features of learning that will continue to be embraced throughout their life. Because once this is achieved, you can know that you have helped them in the best way possible to prepare for their transition.

With dramatic impact on their achievements in the long run, the enriched experiences you offer to children throughout their early years have deep-rooted lasting effects. They are so important in fact, that we will explore them in great detail throughout the final chapters of this book, as I have done with every book in this series. Whilst these are seen in their independence, their confidence and social skills from day one, they are more deeply felt than any individual achievement. You are also developing a child's attitudes towards learning and their perception of their place within it – something that is not easily measured in an observation today but will have monumental impact on all their tomorrows. So, have fun as you engage, discover and marvel at this wonderful world together.

Support your children as they remain motivated learners

Motivation is so important within every child's learning journey and is something they have in great supply when they are very young. Rooted in working towards a goal, motivation is all about retaining the belief that your actions are going to result in you achieving what you have set out to do. When a child was learning to feed themselves, they never gave up no matter how many times the spoon missed its target. But as their goals become a little more complex, we need to be mindful that a child still retains the faith they have that they can achieve them.

If we surround our children with rules and expectations, with little or no power to influence events within their lives, they are unlikely to set goals or attempt to achieve them, becoming content with conforming within the life they are given. This is unfortunately what can happen when children move from freely accessing the things they are driven towards and instead, are expected to find the deep levels of motivation required to persevere with some complex demands of someone else's choosing. So, how can you best support your children now in ways that they can continue to flourish, even after they have left the free play of their early years and have entered the school classroom? As I have explored in previous books in this series, retaining a child's motivation is all about them having the confidence that the efforts they are making will ultimately be worthwhile. To achieve this, you need to look to ways that you can support a child's confidence in their abilities through offering activities they can achieve in.

■ Tasks that will require some continued motivation to see success

■ Tasks that require some problem solving and perseverance

- Challenges that closely match their current levels of ability

- Freedoms to push themselves into new areas

- Allowance to choose what interests them

- Time to lose themselves in engrossing and challenging activities

One study into motivated working looked at artists at work. As it noticed their complete absorption as they lost track of time and self-consciousness, they saw artists becoming entirely immersed in the creative process. What's more, the study also noted that when people have something this exhilarating and profoundly satisfying in their lives, the happier they tended to be. Engagement is more than a willingness to discover, learn and grow; it implies a deep interest and involvement in something considered to be worth the effort. So, think together with your children as you consider what this might mean for them with the resources and authentic problems that make this an interesting experience.

Hands-on learning

There is a reason why so many pedagogical approaches in early education make deliberate use of children's natural inclination to explore using real-world materials. You can tap into a child's innate methods of learning with opportunities to be physical, to follow their interests and to be confident in what they are achieving. You can support these processes, but let your children experience what it means to direct their own learning, exploring what interests them and in the ways they want to, playing with the experiences that they need.

Figure 9.4 How does the weight of this sponge change when I dip it in the water? Where has the water gone? Why are some of my animals floating while others don't? A few simple resources can spark a multitude of investigations.

Provided you recognise, value and understand their attempts as they try, you will see some amazing learning taking place (Figure 9.4).

- Offer creative environments where they can experience things in real terms

- Allow them opportunities to practice different techniques

- Let them use authentic tools and resources

- Offer different experiences of social encounters

- Establish different kinds of problems to solve

Through these experiences you are building a sense of their personal achievement from their own efforts. This is a stabile variable that they can control, rather than focusing on outcomes which may take a while to perfect and therefore seem out of their control.

Preparing everyone for the school classroom

As you help your children and their families prepare for this important transition, be mindful of the anxieties that may already be in place. We are all a product of our experiences and for some, experiences of the school classroom were not enjoyable ones. That is not to say that those who do not succeed in the school classroom do not succeed in life. Some of our best-known entrepreneurs are famous for having disliked classroom learning and have gone on to achieve amazing things. Falling out of love with the classroom might not stunt a child's potential. However, falling out of love with enquiry, of wanting to know, to achieve and to understand just might – especially when this comes with losing confidence in their own abilities. So, the most important thing that we can do for all our children at this time is to instil a love of learning, in all its forms, that they can retain throughout the years to come.

- Recognise and understand the implications of the style of learning and teaching that you are offering

- Encourage free choice and play as central components of learning

- Ensure children have time every day for physical play

- Consider following a project-based approach where children can work on activities of their choosing

- Appreciate the benefits of a less-structured approach

- Be mindful of emotional engagement, ensuring environments are free from adverse stress

- Avoid any suggestion of failing at a task when it is not yet perfected or unintentionally introduce pressures to conform

- Allow children to have an opinion, a thought and a voice

- Allow them to experience the consequences that some of their ideas may come with

Research consistently highlights that children who are playing are learning. Indeed, they are learning things that cannot be mastered while sitting quietly, following the moment-to-moment instructions of a teacher. Imagine the last time you learnt a new skill. Did you do it just by being told, or did you have a go, physically getting involved and exploring what you could do and perfecting ways in which you could do it?

As you integrate these approaches in the early years, do not lose sight of their importance throughout our lives of learning. Picture the most innovative adult-learning environment where real breakthroughs are occurring and significant real-world problems are being solved. These are environments where great minds are sharing their ideas, discussing and brainstorming a way forward, where adults are playing with concepts, exploring rather than simply studying them. As children engage with different experiences, you can be on hand to support them if they struggle with the abstract concepts they are learning about, but avoid taking the struggle away from them. The potential sense of achievement is a gift you do not want to deny them. These are tremendously empowering experiences and in the early years we have such potential to offer these to our children. This can become harder to achieve once they transition into the school classroom, so take full advantage while you have the opportunity to do so.

Note

1 https://www.gov.uk/government/publications/performing-against-the-odds-developmental-trajectories-of-children-in-the-eppse-3-to-16-study

10 Supporting lifelong learning in the years before school

As we have seen, a child's early years are a critical and highly sensitive period of integrated development and rapid growth. This is precious time that no amount of future interventions can make up for. But now, with the start of school looming on the horizon, thoughts can become focused on academic preparation and concerns regarding the discrete skills and abilities that have been mastered. While these are great if a child has been interested in doing these things, they certainly should not be the focus of your attention. As the nature of support children need is changing, all adults within a child's life need to be aware of the diverse and deeply important development that continues to occur. And while some of this support will be focused on their transition into formal education, there is much more going on besides.

When a child is given opportunities to do things for themselves, their independence and self-motivation can flourish. With opportunities to push their own limits and take risks, a courageous and confident attitude to future possibilities can develop. When they are able to have a go for themselves and experience new things, this allows their curiosity to ignite, along with a multitude of physical and mental abilities as they're establishing the memories that all future learning will rely on (Figure 10.1). As children embed these features of lifelong learning, their experiences in the school classroom are being shaped far more significantly than when developing their knowledge of the alphabet. But even more profoundly, through these experiences children are also developing their attitudes towards learning and their

Figure 10.1 Capturing a child's imagination is a far more powerful influence on their success at school than any amount of numbers or letters you are teaching them at this age.

DOI: 10.4324/9781003327042-11

perception of how well they are suited to it. And none of this stops just because the school classroom is approaching.

Children are learning from the moment they are born, with every experience informing their response to the next. And those they are having during their first years of life, with you, are fundamental. But for reasons more deeply felt than actively preparing them for formal learning and the school classroom. With their personalities and abilities growing daily, they are developing deep-rooted characteristics that are forming not only the learner, but the person they will become.

In this chapter we will then look at the learning opportunities you are offering and how these nurture a GIFTED Learning approach. So, whether you are new to this set of books or familiar with them, look at how you can engage children in their learning as you embrace this period of greater physical and mental ability, of independence and awareness of the world around them. Learn to focus your attention on their developing dispositions and responses towards learning opportunities during this formative period. All the while remember that early childhood must be viewed as something far more important than a PRE-school, but as an Early Years with its own unique importance as you take every opportunity to engage, discover and marvel together.

Knowledge

Know how children's approaches to learning are maturing and how this needs rooting in appropriate challenge and opportunity if abilities, rather than facts, are going to give children the start they need

The strength of a child's ability to learn is embedded from the moment of birth. Born highly motivated to know, to understand and to perfect their repertoire of skills, they are eager to make the most of any and every opportunity. How else would they master the fantastic transformation they have had from the baby they were just a few years ago? If you think of how much they now know, the skills they have perfected and the behaviours they have learnt, their learning journey and the proficiency that has developed through it has been monumental. And yet soon after formal learning begins, children are often found to disengage from learning, possibly announcing that they are bored or that they do not like school. This is a tragic state of affairs and one that needs immediate and universal attention.

When you are involved in a child's life during these foundational years you are doing so much more than getting them ready to transition into a school classroom. Through every enriched early childhood experience steeped in rich vocabulary, practical activities and social play you are shaping all their tomorrows. The influence of this could not be more pronounced. Not only are you laying the foundations of all their future learning, but you are also creating the person they are going to be as well as instilling the personal beliefs they have in themselves to strive forward and achieve.

Within this process we have a duty to our children to prepare them for a future none of us can envision fully, wherever that may take them. Yes academically, but also socially, emotionally and as an inspired, eager human being ready for anything. Within this environment, a child can feel recognised, valued and esteemed. They learn that they can communicate openly with a voice of their own as you show them the importance of responsibility, honesty and ownership. And through your care they will develop a sense of who they are in the world, ready for when they go out into it. The trouble is this process can often become misguided or confused when it is not well understood, and this can have devastating effects on the development of a child at a time when their interest in the world and all it has to offer is just beginning.

Figure 10.2 In every moment you are showing a child what it means to learn something new. As you take advantage of their greater interest in the world, their growing mental abilities and independent thought, open up a world of new discoveries for them.

Developing a child's full potential

Ask yourself, where have your greatest accomplishments in life come from? Have these been in the areas that have been expected of you or the things that you have been interested in pursuing? And how many of the former have you abandoned along the way? When we offer children first-hand, spontaneous experiences, we capture their natural instincts for leaning. We show them that they are in a nurturing environment where their thoughts and ideas are heard and understood from their earliest days (Figure 10.2).

- Now that their physical abilities are maturing, they need opportunities to stretch their muscles, to climb, spin and leap more than they need to sit still on a carpet

- As their social skills are developing, they need activities that encourage them to communicate, to work together and share ideas – not to simply listen to one voice

- As their awareness of the world is developing, they need the ability to explore their interests in it rather than following the interests somebody else thought of, possibly some time ago

But this needs an element of trust. If you want your children to develop to their full potential, you need to give them the space, time and autonomy to discover it. You need to allow them to develop the learnt behaviours that will see them strive for the things they want. And as you nurture the instincts that underpin this work, do so while valuing the independent thinkers you have in front of you. Allow them to push their limits with enough interest and commitment to do so.

When we facilitate children's opportunities to rehearse, challenge and adapt their thinking we allow them to explore their knowledge and understanding, learning the benefits of perseverance and curiosity as they develop the ability to think in creative and logical ways. And it is in instilling these features of lifelong learning that we must focus on as we think about what early learning means to a child. So, as you recognise the importance of child-initiated free play, be sure to encourage and utilise all the opportunities you have around you and look to nurture these deep-rooted processes of learning through every opportunity.

Meaningful learning through play

Throughout early childhood, it is important that we remember the huge range of growth and development that is occurring and the impact this foundational period is having on children. And the best – and quite frankly only – way to do this is though meaningful play, facilitated, not governed, by adults who understand the value of these rich and diverse experiences.

As we have seen, children are trying out various roles as they play, initiating and manipulating experiences as they see how something beyond their means or capabilities feels. As they play with various resources, investigating and making decisions on what they will do next, they are exploring the power of an idea and what can come from it. When they hit difficulties or make a mistake, they are learning what it means to persist, to try again and to apply new ways of thinking. All of these are powerfully important methods children use to make sense of their world, but these are not things you can know in advance or plan an activity to manage. Instead, your children need you to know how important these opportunities are. They need you to facilitate their access to an enriched environment that they are free to engage with in the moment, utilising their whole bodies as they explore their ideas and insights. You might like to observe them during the day with these questions in mind.

- Will they have the time and space they need to fully explore their own ideas?

- Can they follow their own agenda and pursue their discoveries in different ways?

- Are they allowed to combine different resources and concepts?

- Can they move into whichever areas they need to as an idea occurs to them?

- Does this include moving outdoors too?

Understanding

Understand the deep-rooted learning that children's opportunities and available resources need to offer them during these years

As you are no doubt aware from your own experiences of learning anything new, success has as much to do with self-belief as it does with any level of intelligence you might possess. During their enormously influential early years, your children are sharing so many experiences of learning with you. But what can be overlooked are their first experiences of what it means to try to learn. Every experience is teaching them something about the impact of their actions and whether the effort they are putting in is worth their while.

Through each experience children are learning to view the world in their own unique and highly personal ways and it is important that these processes are respected. We can do this by recognising the deep level thinking and reflections that they are demonstrating through their behaviours, even when their responses may be different to what we were expecting. We can support a child's journey by listening when they say something unexpected, ready to explore their thoughts, valuing the unusual responses that are offered and discovering the unique opinions that any reaction is demonstrating. As you facilitate this level of thinking, you are giving the thought process the respect that comes from your interest and recognition, while you have the personal knowledge and opportunity to do so – and you are showing a child that their thoughts are worthy of development and persisting with. Only then can you nurture the depth of learning they are capable of.

This speaks of GIFTED Learning. Introduced in the first book in this series, *Nurturing Babies* and further developed in *Nurturing Toddlers*, GIFTED Learning looks at the Greater Involvement Facilitated Through Engaging in Dispositions and is the first stage of the Theory of Lifelong Development (ToLD), which I will continue to revisit throughout this series of books.

Understand the importance of GIFTED Learning

GIFTED Learning recognises that if we want our children to learn, they need to be motivated to do so. They need to be able to think, to communicate and to adapt to new ideas. They need to have courage in themselves and their eventual success if their efforts are going to seem worthwhile. They need to be imaginative, curious and reflective and a whole bunch of other dispositions that all need opportunities to be developed. And this can only happen when children have the time, permissions and resources that result in positive experiences. This doesn't mean that everything works out perfectly first time, but it does mean that their attempts are recognised, facilitated and valued. Because if they aren't, children begin to disengage, when they had every opportunity for their world to ignite.

When we recognise the impact we have on our children's lifelong learning and development trajectories through their dispositional engagement, we begin to understand the importance of them. In previous books in this series, I have acknowledged that this may sound complex and involve terms you may not be familiar with. However, children are complex and trying to smooth out their multilayered complexity does everyone a disservice – and good luck trying! However, through these books you will learn everything you need to nurture GIFTED learning for all your children, now and throughout a lifetime of learning.

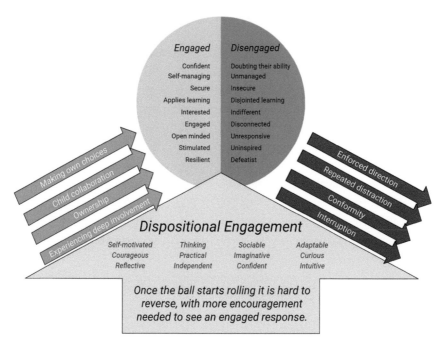

GIFTED Learning
Greater Involvement Facilitated Through Engaging in Dispositions

Figure 10.3 GIFTED Learning This speaks of retaining children's engagement in the learning process and asks you to notice what happens to a child when you take their potential for engagement away.

Let us take another look then at the importance of GIFTED Learning now that our focus is on a child older than we have considered in previous books. Once again I will stress here that you will find no age categories or expectations; children are continuously learning and developing, in holistic and deeply individual ways. As they are affected by their environment, the people in it, the autonomy they are given to engage and every experience that has gone before, this cannot be neatly split into "learning areas" or "focused" activities. Instead, we must keep our attentions focused on the child in front of us, in this moment, rather than any tick sheet we are trying to align them with.

So, every time you engage with a child, be aware of how you are impacting the development of these dispositions through the messages you inadvertently send. Consider the world of possibilities you can explore as you avoid unfulfilling activities. Instead, value the unexpected as you help children to engage in their dispositions, learning through every unusual or unexpected teachable moment (Figure 10.3).

Are you giving your children learning superpowers?
Children are born eager to learn and understand their world. And they are hard-wired to utilise and develop these dispositions to become better at it. However, soon

classroom experiences of learning are going to replace many of the freedoms of experience that you now enjoy. When this happens, children may find limited opportunities to use their natural methods of learning, unable to pursue an idea for as long as they need, to be autonomous in the decisions they are making or to access the resources or environments that will allow them to explore an idea fully. Now is your opportunity to embrace these styles of learning as you give children opportunities to demonstrate their developing dispositions within experiences matched to their needs.

Let them think about why the properties of a shape might be important or imagine different ways of using sounds to communicate with each other. Allow children to be independent as they self-direct and explore their own direction of enquiry, reflecting on what they have done, using their intuition and revisiting as often as needed. Talk with them as you consider a dilemma in a social group, helping the less confident to find their voice. When you take the time to genuinely engage, showing your interest, you show that you trust in their efforts that are meaningful and worth pursuing. And be sure to see any lack of knowledge, yours as well as theirs, as areas to be explored. Through diverse practical and authentic experiences, encourage discussion as they trial and approach new ideas and let them see and feel the impact of their learning as their ideas take shape, avoiding the sense of failure that its premature removal or over direction could otherwise introduce.

Any negative, or seemingly meaningless, experiences of learning will soon be viewed as futile by a child and are likely to have an impact on their future levels of effort. This will impact their potential achievement, both directly as they lose interest in the process of learning and through its effect on their self-confidence, their motivations and tendency to think for themselves, all of which you will see reflected in their attention skills, concentration and persistence.

Instead, allow children to get stuck into the learning process; measuring the flour rather than watching you do it, waiting for a token stir. Offer them access to adaptable, multisensory and authentic items as you promote and extend their investigations, being sure to provide the right tools for the job. Offer children the resources and permissions they need to explore tricky concepts, including fantasy and risky play. As they use these to explore their emotions and complex social interactions, embrace the opportunity to react to their evolving interests and any unexpected events.

As you offer children these rich activities, avoid becoming focused on getting the task done or achieving its desired learning objectives and think instead of the journey the child is on. If you think for a moment about what draws you to something you love to do – a sport you enjoy, reading a favourite author or becoming lost in a film – this is not about getting through as many as possible, ticking them off a list, but the deep enjoyment you take from the moments you are lost in doing these activities. To a child, these moments of being absorbed in their play offers them this. As we look to establish the best possible start for our children, it is important that we keep these motivations close to mind as they retain their curiosity and desire to learn. Let them decide what activities will offer this and perhaps question the sense of endlessly naming shapes or repeating the sound of the day. After all, we all remember school and being told what you must do and read next; it can suck all the fun out of learning.

Developing a love of learning

A child's emotional engagement to their learning is also a deeply important part of the process. Any attempts at systematically downloading knowledge into the minds of developing children is simply counterproductive. And when unnecessary stress is added to the experience, these events can become linked in the child's mind. If pressures to conform or to respond in ways they are not yet developmentally ready for are then added to the mix, the whole process of learning may become associated with negativity, a link that becomes more firmly established with each experience. Eventually, an expectation or fear of failure may see a child look to avoid the styles of learning those have been experienced within, with behaviours that may read as disruptive or be misunderstood as a lack of ability.

Developing the executive functioning of successful thinkers

When we offer children activities that can be completed in any number of ways, we are giving them ownership of their thoughts and ideas. We are suggesting that different approaches are perfectly feasible; that there is not simply one right way to do something while everything else is somehow wrong. This approach also suggests that mistakes can be made and that trialling alternative methods is a worthwhile endeavour on our way to perfection.

When we offer children activities with multiple steps that involve the management of a range of tasks, this requires some complex processing. To be successful at this means a child must keep these different steps in their head for as long as it takes to act on them appropriately – focusing on them in the right order, understanding when one thing has to happen before another and being able to mentally tick them off as they are completed. And within every opportunity a child has to engage in activities with other children, whether this is as a pair or in a small group, their social skills are being challenged and developed. Where resources are shared and success requires the cooperation and perhaps support of a friend, the benefit of collaborative working is being demonstrated, alongside the importance of managing any self-serving impulses.

To get good or even comfortable with doing all these things takes practice. But these skills are rooted in many of the playful activities we can offer to children. As you see your children's cognitive flexibility, working memory and self-control flourish, know you are offering far more important abilities than working towards any learning objectives you may have started the day with. You are offering developmental processes that are essential to their mental and physical health, as well as all their future learning and educational attainment. Remember, children aren't born with these executive skills, but they are born with the potential to develop them.

Support

Be supported in implementing lifelong learning in the years before school and helping all the key adults in their life to do the same

A child's methods of learning and understanding their world have not changed, even if our understanding and focus has. To make the deep-rooted connections they need within their learning, a child needs to touch and manipulate the world around them. They need opportunities to experiment with their ideas as they explore new concepts, freely introducing and combining new resources. They need time to intellectually process, access, practice and explore as they make the deep-rooted connections between the areas of understanding they are gaining. If you can provide your children with creative environments and tangible experiences, their intrinsic motivation, curiosity and independence will bloom.

- Support their curiosity by linking authentic toys to experiences within the home and then their immediate environment

- Use realistic items to embrace their culture, explore their own identity and the people and experienced realities around them

- Allow your children to own their environment, able to freely access and manipulate the resources and to change things as they need

- Offer familiar, genuine experiences that children can find a greater interest in and become more satisfied by

And when you can support this with an awareness of what your children know and what they want to know, you can offer it within the environments and opportunities your children need.

GIFTED Learning is rooted in good communication

A child's ability to make a productive start in the school classroom is determined more through the opportunities they have had for communication during their early years than any other factor. Imagine for one moment the experiences being faced by a child with limited language within the realities of your environment. Then compare this to the head start experienced by a confident speaker. If you then fast forward this comparison into the school classroom, the resulting outcomes and social dynamics are clear.

Problems may begin straight away as a child is assumed to be overly introverted or shy as they seem to show a reluctance to get involved, when in reality they are simply lacking the communication skills to do so. Alternatively they may appear extroverted as they use less vocal, yet perhaps more dramatic means of having an impact on the group. Either way, feelings of frustration are likely to develop in them and the wider group, and in both scenarios, potential isolation may soon follow. Unchecked, this may see lower rates of cooperation or conformity, disruption or disobedience as lower displays of cognitive development become confused with lower ability.

It is then important that you support all children's access to rich, two-way dialogue with every opportunity within real social interactions, where language and communication development continue to be your key focus.

- Encourage social interactions, discussion and collaboration with you, with other children and with other adults as you support and enrich their social, emotional and cognitive achievements

- Consider activities together, as you explore gaps or investigate misunderstandings

- Allow children to consider the resources and planning they might need for a task together; be inspired by their interests and enthusiasms as you let them guide you

- Avoid dictating or leading their play with your expectations

- Take measures to prevent motivated play being interrupted wherever you can

Staging GIFTED Learning environments

Children are active and independent thinkers who learn best when allowed to combine many processes as their learning flourishes. Allow your children to access and repeat the experiences they need when they need them and how they need them. Offer diverse ranges of practical, authentic experiences within different social groupings. Promote their language development as you offer opportunities to discuss, trial and approach new ideas where logical steps and lateral thinking can be explored. Supply requested information rather than all the answers as you allow them to find their voice and reflect on their past actions and achievements (Figure 10.4). Once you recognise and respect that every child will view the world in unique and highly personal ways, you can develop their diverse

Figure 10.4 Genuine engagement comes when we give children authentic, hands-on experiences of getting stuck in.

methods of thinking and reflection, promoting the meaningful levels of understanding they will need for symbolic and abstract thought and to go beyond a surface level of knowledge.

- Maximise children's opportunities by considering the dispositions they are developing

- Identify areas that are receiving limited attention and talk with children about activities that might address this

- Take every opportunity to explore new experiences that touch on all areas of engagement

- Help them see lack of knowledge as areas that still need to be explored, rather than as having reached a barrier in their learning

- Offer the time and opportunity for children to self-direct, revisiting areas as often as needed

- Trust in a child's judgement of what they can and want to do as you celebrate their uniquely developing efforts

- Take play outside for increased stimulation and freedom

- Allow children time and space to ponder and wallow, losing themselves in their enquiries as they explore ideas, concepts, feelings, emotions and behaviours

- And don't forget, sensory learning is still as powerful now as it was when they were a baby

Resources should be:

- Fresh, interesting and stimulating, capturing attention, generating ideas and challenging thinking

- Plentiful so they can be explored in various ways

- Open ended rather than manufactured for a purpose, where a predetermined goal may limit investigation and deeper learning

- Be thought-provoking, encouraging discussion, questioning and investigating their purpose, ensuring you are not automatically the "expert"

Children also need to feel positive about the efforts they make. Within rich experiences children can see the results of their efforts as their opinions about working towards a goal and their belief in their own abilities are established. As this is happening, offer meaningful, measured and focused praise arising from the effort they are putting in. Focus on a variable they control as you strengthen their motivation in the long term. As I have explored in previous books in this series, the alternative serves to undervalue persistence, causing children to give up when greater challenges are faced. Challenges encountered, they assume, because they are "not clever enough" rather than they need to apply more effort. But watch first, be careful not to interrupt a key moment of engagement and wait for those natural breaks or when they turn to you for reassurance.

- Let children see something real come of something they have talked about as you enhance their connections and add personal relevance to their reflections

- Within safe environments, allow them to play out disputes rather than using distraction or simply telling them to "Stop" as they learn how to rationalise and talk through conflicts, trailing techniques and solving their own problems

- Offer your children opportunities to be courageous and confident through achievable challenges

- Invite them to use their imagination and intuition, solving problems and making decisions as they demonstrate and celebrate their individual ideas, unafraid of making mistakes and keen to try again

- Support this process with initial links to what is familiar. Bring familiar songs, rhymes and books to life with genuine objects, then present a new object that together you structure a story around.

Section 2
Introduction
The Nurturing Childhoods Pedagogical Framework

Key Features of The Nurturing Childhoods Pedagogical Framework

In the first book in this series, *Nurturing Babies*, I introduced you to the Nurturing Childhoods Pedagogical Framework (NCPF) and the notion of GIFTED Learning. In the second book, *Nurturing Toddlers*, we turned our attention to more mobile children with greater autonomy and I added the ABCs of Developing Engagement (ABCoDE). Now, as we consider children with a few more years of learning experiences behind them, I will add a method that will allow you to look at the impact these experiences are having on your children (Figure S2.1).

KEY FEATURES OF THE
Nurturing Childhoods Framework

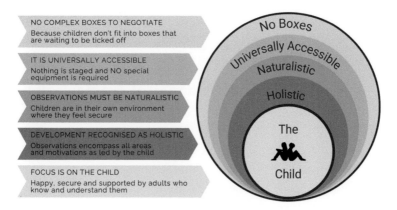

Figure S2.1 The Nurturing Childhoods Framework is unique for its central focus on the developing child, rather than any learning goals that serve only to draw focus away.

DOI: 10.4324/9781003327042-12

Then, in the final book in this series, *Nurturing Children through the Primary Years*, as we turn our attention to practices within more formalised environments, I will introduce you to techniques that demonstrate the impact of a range of variables on a child's engaged experiences. But first let us take another look at the key features of the Nurturing Childhoods Pedagogical Framework.

As I have mentioned in all the books in this series, the first thing to notice is that the Framework positions children, rather than any early learning goals or targets, at the centre of our thinking as we bring our focus back where it belongs. It acknowledges the need to focus on a child's well-being and sense of security before looking to any higher-order demands and stresses the need for adults who know and understand them.

From here it recognises that a child's development is holistic, infinitely connected and constantly evolving through processes that cannot be neatly pigeon-holed and, instead, need opportunities for a child to feel a sense of agency and control. But in order to nurture this development, we must look to the environments and the sense of belonging they offer. We must be mindful of our interactions, our body language and the permissions and tone we convey. All of this is dependent on the children, the families and realities that surround us.

To that end there can be no suggested delivery, no requirement for specialist equipment or specific locations. There are no narrowly defined expectations, targets, lesson plans or agendas and you certainly won't be looking to fit children into any boxes. Instead, the Framework asks us to look at the behaviours and actions of a child as we learn to understand the messages they send us, remaining aware of what these behaviours are telling us about the opportunities we are offering and how these allow children to think for themselves, to make choices and participate as well as the deeper learning processes that are taking root, the characteristics that are developing and the dispositions underpinning their responses.

As a pedagogy it runs alongside any statutory curriculum or framework, offering an additional lens to understand children's actions and behaviours through. This then means that it is not about to change with a new government initiative or change of approach. Nor does it matter where in the world you are regulated, or even the year you are reading these words. Nurturing practice is both universal and timeless.

The Nurturing Childhoods Pedagogical Framework (NCPF)

In previous books in this series I have asked you to look at children's development in ways you may have been less familiar with. In *Nurturing Babies*, when I introduced you to the NCPF, we situated the child at the centre of our thinking. Rather than focusing on learning goals or developmental milestones, essentially driving from an adult perspective, we looked instead at children's behaviours as our responses are driven from the child.

Recognising the importance of behaviours, both in terms of how they demonstrate the affordances we offer to children and, in turn, how they communicate their responses back to us, the NCPF has allowed us to recognise children as holistic learners influenced at once by the environment surrounding them and the relationships that have been established, as well as every experience leading up to the moment you are now observing.

In *Nurturing Toddlers*, as we explored how the greater freedoms of movement and conscious desires are now affecting the behaviours being demonstrated, I introduced the ABCoDE. Recognising that the behaviours demonstrated by a toddler are more directly influenced by the child than they were a few months ago, the ABCoDE (Figure S2.2) reminds us of the importance of nurturing behaviours and the developing characteristics they reveal.

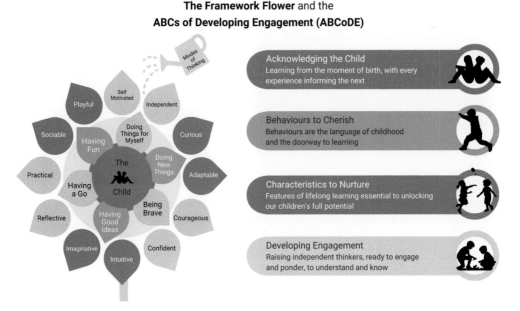

Figure S2.2 The Framework Flower and the ABCs of Developing Engagement (ABCoDE). Sitting alongside the Nurturing Childhoods Pedagogical Framework and acting as an additional lens through which to view it, the ABCs of Developing Engagement (ABCoDE) helps us to look at children's deep-rooted developments firstly through ACKNOWLEDGING the child and all that they are, then through observing their BEHAVIOURS or what is often termed the language of childhood, whilst remaining mindful of the developing CHARACTERISTICS that are underpinning them.

Whether you are familiar with this framework or it is your first experience of it, you will notice how it focuses our understanding of learning by noticing children's behaviours, sometimes described as the *"language of childhood"*. Through these behaviours we can then learn a great deal about the developing characteristics of the child and their dispositions towards certain responses, the importance of which you will remember from Chapter 10, when we looked at GIFTED Learning and how we can facilitate greater involvement in the learning process when we understand and enable our children's engagement in the dispositions that are fundamental to it. With the ABCoDE sitting alongside the NCPF, acting as an additional lens through which to view it, it helps us look at children's deep-rooted developments. Focusing on THIS child, in THIS moment, in THIS environment, mindful of everything that may imply.

Now, as our children are approaching their third, fourth, fifth and sixth years, they have a few more years' worth of experiences informing these behaviours and the trajectories their dispositions are developing on is becoming more pronounced. This can be a positive process, as every experience leads to more confident, self-motivated and imaginative learners. Or these can become negative, self-conscious, reluctant and closed-off character traits, influenced by any negative or limiting experiences the child may find themselves in. During this highly pivotal period of development, as freedoms of movement increase, voices establish and social collaborations intensify, we must be aware of what a child's behaviours are telling us about these trajectories and how they are establishing.

Introducing the OPTED Scale

To this end I would now like to introduce you to the OPTED Scale, which you can think of simply as "what are your children opting to do?" The Observed Preference Towards Engaging in a Disposition Scale (adapted from the FOLLEP Scale) was devised to support my own research into children's engagements (Peckham, 2021). Heavily influenced by Farre Laevers and his work with well-being and engagement scales, the OPTED Scale allows us to observe the full range of developing characteristics quickly and easily, whilst remaining mindful of the different environments, pedagogies and provocations that influence this process. It also allows us to reflect on a child's behaviours over time in a holistic and continual way as they demonstrate their tendencies to engage – or retreat – from certain characteristics, indicating their developing tendencies towards them.

The OPTED Scale is a five-point scale that allows you to quickly and easily gauge a child's involvement in any one of the NCPF characteristics (Figure S2.3). A rating of zero sits at the middle of this scale, where there is no opportunity or inclination towards this characteristic in this moment. Moving upwards, an observation can record a +1 for some indication or a +2 if the child is showing a clear indication of being engaged in this way. Moving downwards, an observation can also indicate −1 if a child demonstrates some reluctance towards this characteristic or −2 if, in this moment, they actively pull away, showing a clear disinclination.

The first thing to note about the OPTED Scale is that it is used to record an OBSERVATION, not a CHILD. So, while during an observation on a Tuesday afternoon in March you may record confidence with a −2, there could be many factors affecting this. However, when you repeat this observation you find you are frequently recording confidence at −2, this may tell you something about how this child's

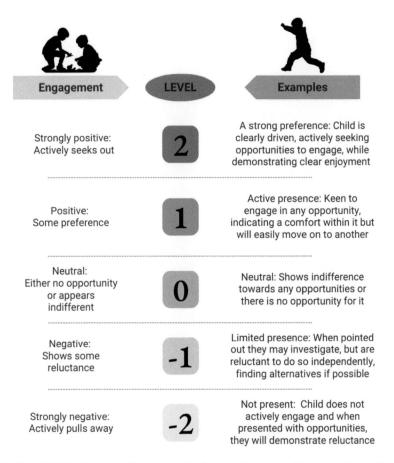

Figure S2.3 The OPTED Scale – Observed Preference Towards Engaging in a Disposition.
The OPTED Scale allows you to understand what you are seeing at a deeper level and offers ways of tracking the impact of your decisions on all of these processes.

disposition towards being confident is developing. It might also tell you something about the opportunities you are offering children to be brave. Equally it could tell you a lot about the activities scheduled on a Tuesday afternoon or the staff on rota. So, let me repeat, this scale is used to illustrate a child's preference as they engage in a range of dispositions in this moment; it is not a label we affix to the child.

Because of its versatility it can then be used to monitor developing trends towards engagement, the development of dispositions, even the environment, activities and adult behaviours that enable them. However, with every experience we have informing our next, these trends are of great importance. If a child is reluctant to show confidence this Tuesday afternoon, they will use this memory to inform their next responses to an opportunity to be confident. If this was a one-off, it will have little impact. However, if this is a trend you are seeing developing, for any number of reasons, negative trajectories could be establishing.

To illustrate this further, in the next book in the series I will introduce you to techniques that allow you to monitor OPTED Scales through a range of variables as these become more adult governed for children through the primary years.

But for now we will explore each of the six observable behaviours illustrated in the NCPF and the dispositions underpinning them. We'll finish with a look at the modes of thinking that unite them all. We will look at their importance, how we can develop a child's abilities and desires to explore them and the practices, environments and experiences that facilitate them now that we are looking at the abilities and motivations of a more self-directed child. I did this for babies in the first book and toddlers in the second and will look at children in the school classroom in the next book in this series. That said, you will notice a distinct lack of monthly age boundaries or expectations. This framework applies to all learners, regardless of age, and whilst your attention needs to adapt in line with the child in front of you, the framework and its ability to support and nurture our children's development remains constant.

So, as we go through these next chapters, I invite you to think of a young child you know well. If one doesn't easily come to mind, think of yourself as a young child and embrace this call to arms as we actively help raise this awareness for all our children.

Reference

Peckham, K. (2021) A phenomenological study exploring how early childhood pedagogies enable the development of dispositions. Doctoral thesis, Birmingham City University.

Nurturing young children to do things for themselves

Doing Things For Myself
BECOMING SELF-MOTIVATED AND INDEPENDENT

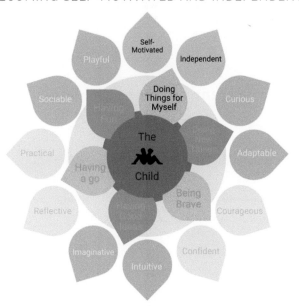

Figure 11.1 Doing Things For Myself – Becoming Self-Motivated and Independent. When we nurture a young child's opportunities to do things for themselves, they develop the self-motivation and sense of independence that allows them to do it for themselves next time.

In this chapter we are going to focus our attentions on nurturing young children as they do things for themselves, developing the self-motivation and the sense of independence that allows them to do so (Figure 11.1).

As children's cognitive reasoning and thinking skills are developing, the processes being utilised are becoming more complex. For these developments to happen

DOI: 10.4324/9781003327042-13

effectively, children need to have their attention captured in ways that are consistent enough to have lasting impact. When this happens, their level of interest and self-motivation is high enough for them to persevere with an activity long enough for it to have an impact and for these experiences to result in lasting pleasurable memories of self-motivated discovery and achievement. This is not going to happen from them watching other people do something but from getting opportunities to try these things for themselves.

When they have had experiences of doing things for themselves, children develop a sense of self-sufficiency and security within their ability to do something. Through these opportunities they can develop a level of confidence in their own eventual success, independent of external influences. When they encounter barriers or difficulties, they will then know that they have the capacity to pull through. And they have learnt to see the difficulties they encounter as potential for new discoveries rather than as a reason for giving up. Through these experiences, a child's self-motivation and independence is flourishing in ways that can see their full potential realised.

Knowledge

Know why it is important for young children to do things for themselves

As children become more able to take on tasks for themselves, they can seem to become overwhelmed by the possibilities on offer, starting one thing only to move on to another and then to something else. This is a perfectly natural response to their changing abilities and growing minds as they explore this sense of independence and the things that interest them. They will be learning "just in time" rather than "just in case", moving around the space as they acquire the deep knowledge they need when it interests them.

This is far more powerful than any planned learning for some future need. But this needs independent access to a wide range of meaningful experiences as children become engaged in their own autonomous learning without being unnecessarily led or interrupted (Figure 11.2).

With every experience of trying something new, children are gaining more than the experiences in the moment. They are establishing a sense of what they are capable of and through this, a personal belief in themselves as a competent learner. How well these moments are experienced

Figure 11.2 The enjoyment in the moment and the memories being created are far more important than any learning objective you may have had.

are then more important than any realised outcomes, as their self-motivation within all future learning develops.

Given opportunities to do things for themselves, children can become completely absorbed in an activity, establishing positive emotional reactions towards their learning and the wider thought processes involved. However, when their investigations become led by adult questions or preplanned directions, children can become restless and seemingly exhausted by the process. They may tend to give up quickly, even when they know what they should be doing or are quick to seek help. However, when a sense of independence and self-motivation is offered, free of time pressures or expectations, children may construct new meaning from experiencing their own independent enquiries, becoming more inclined to try next time.

Understanding

Understand how to develop a young child's ability and desire to do things for themselves

You can help children to become more self-sufficient by offering them opportunities to experience their success. Let them take the lead in directing an activity, rather than simply following the ideas you may have previously had. And avoid becoming overly concerned for a desired or expected outcome. When you can relax your expectations of a learning experience and allow the child to direct its outcomes, the chances are these will be far richer than you would have imagined.

Supported with the right opportunities, some inspiring resources and the space and time to investigate, children can experience the benefits of persisting with a task. Their deep-rooted self-motivation can then establish, ready for times in their future learning when external motivations may be lacking. These will not be as pronounced in tasks of your choosing or where they do not see a purpose, so allow them to set their own agenda through their play as their natural motivations are ignited. This may then lead to a need for other skills, such as writing a note or understanding a number, which you can help them with.

This "just in time" learning is hugely purposeful and rewarding. But take care to ensure that this motivated play is not derailed by any unnecessary interruptions, expectations or adult direction. Instead, let them realise the benefits of persisting as they experience their success. When you would ordinarily intervene or enforce a break to the activity, pause a moment and consider if it is really necessary. Is it needed? Is it needed now? Could it be done a different way?

To get things started you might like to offer a stimulating object, task or environment, designed to arouse children's interest, possibly to encourage several children to come together and solve a problem, to explore the meaning of something or to understand why. Resist dictating these explorations or interrupting them with unhelpful questioning and instead, stand back and allow the play to evolve. You can be on hand to offer support when they have identified a need for it as you trust in them to know what they need or the direction their explorations need to take next. Take these moments to observe as they ponder their actions and activities. However, avoid feeling the need to get them back on task. Sometimes a moment of quiet contemplation or an alternative source of stimulation is just what is needed and not evidence of a child losing interest or demonstrating a lack of understanding that needs your intervention.

Support

Be supported in offering practice, environments and experiences where this can be explored

As you facilitate children's play and investigations, allow them to experience what it means to decide things for themselves as they begin to take personal ownership of their actions. For some children who are perhaps unfamiliar with any degree of freedom, doing something for themselves may feel a little daunting and you may prefer to start smaller or by offering a choice of what they might like to do next, such as what art materials they might like out or what book they might like before lunch before helping you set this up (Figure 11.3). As they begin to experience the impact of this autonomy within their day, you can extend the possibilities as they decide on possible activities: construction bricks, train tracks or Duplo, a trip to the park or to the field to see the horse?

You can offer them opportunities to plan out and organise their own activities, alone and with friends. Discuss their intentions and gather the resources they think they will need, amending their direction and plans as freely as they need to. This may be completed within moments as they move on to a new task, or take days or even weeks to complete, so be sure to allow all the time it needs, managing all but the necessary interruptions to their motivated engagements and facilitating things so you do not have to keep packing things away.

As you offer lots of authentic opportunities for your children to engage freely in their play, allow them to find their own direction, complete with problems that need solving. This is most effective when their ideas are realised in the moment they occur to them, so try to offer it where you can. While it will not be possible for them to follow every self-motivated impulse, it

Figure 11.3 Giving children opportunities to direct their own challenges and activities offers far more motivation than anything you could plan.

is hugely motivating to a child as they experience doing things for themselves in the moment.

As they experience these self-motivated and independent enquiries, encourage children to identify and seek out whatever information and support they need for themselves. While you can be on hand to support them if this support is being requested, avoid giving them answers they did not identify a need for. As you observe them, only become involved if their activity needs a novel idea or piece of equipment they are unaware of to continue, picking your moment before disturbing their play. In this way children are better able to experience their own success, rather than following your lead. This is far more empowering, with a more motivating impact on later opportunities as they see their own efforts as something worth pursuing and a belief in their own abilities flourish.

12 Nurturing young children to do new things

Doing New Things
BECOMING CURIOUS AND ADAPTABLE

Figure 12.1 Doing New Things – Becoming Curious and Adaptable. When we nurture a young child's opportunities to do new things, they can experience what it means to be curious and adapt to changing circumstances, allowing these dispositions to develop.

In this chapter we are going to focus our attentions on nurturing young children as they do new things, developing the curiosity to want to and the ability to adapt when things change (Figure 12.1).

We want our children to develop the desire to know and understand; to feel inspired to do new things and to embrace the challenges that are important to them. These

DOI: 10.4324/9781003327042-14

processes will come with unforeseen setbacks that require adaptability and a flexible approach. But with these skills in place, children can become capable of embracing opportunities and optimising them as they learn by their experiences rather than becoming anxious or closed off to their potential.

However, deeply rewarding knowledge begins with an element of curiosity, rather than simply learning the things we expect children to know and being adaptable enough to proceed even when things do not go quite as according to plan. When we can inspire curiosity in our children, they are more likely to want to engage. And when we allow them to seek answers to the questions that have occurred to them we can value this curiosity in ways that create long-lasting and reaffirming memories. If children are eager to know how a battery works, how an aircraft can stay in the sky or what life might be like for children in a different country, great opportunities are being offered for them to explore this curiosity as you offer children new experiences of finding things out for themselves.

Knowledge

Know why it is important for young children to do new things

As children get a little older, they will be increasingly introduced to new people, places and experiences. With this increasing maturity comes new opportunities, more diverse social encounters and greater challenges, all of which is fuelling their growing curiosity about the world around them and observing their effects on it. With greater control of their own bodies and more awareness of the other bodies around them, they are also becoming increasingly curious to see what they can achieve. How does this compare with what their friends can do or the things they could do yesterday?

As children become progressively capable of doing things for themselves, they will be keen to try everything. Especially as this belief in their abilities is less dented by reality than it will become in future years. It is then important that we marvel in their sense of curiosity and offer them as much of the growing sense of freedom that they are keen to indulge in as we can, fuelled by their peers, the natural environment and its resources and freer from adult direction and supervision (Figure 12.2).

As they become better able to manage things for themselves, children are keen to follow their own interests and implement their own ideas as they learn the benefits of curious enquiry. Can they return to the fun that was had

Figure 12.2 The adults role is to recognise a child's sense of wonder and to facilitate them as they explore the world, supplying the resources that take a new experience to the next level.

yesterday to see how they can take the experience further? What more can they achieve? How can yesterday's wisdom be tried in a different way? Given these freedoms, a child's curiosity can really bloom as they become increasingly engaged in the things that interest them. And through these diverse experiences, they develop the ability to be flexible as situations change, seeing initial setbacks as simply challenges that need a different solution.

Understand how to develop a young child's ability and desire to do new things

When children are trying lots of new things, they will undoubtedly hit obstacles and difficulties along the way. Their youthful optimism that had them believe they could do anything is being challenged and they may, after a while, seem reluctant to try. The trick to keeping their desire to try new things is then to ensure this remains a positive experience for them, and when difficulties arise, that they have a range of techniques available to face them with.

Firstly, think about the opportunities you can offer and the permissions you can put in place so that a child feels able to trial their ideas as they occur. What control do they have of their environment? Are they able to go outside and see if they can find the bug they have just seen in a book or to trial their ideas for a bridge with the space to design it? How regulated is their day? Is it worth investing the time into trying something new or is this likely to be curtailed before completion? Can they approach their investigations in the ways they feel they need to, or is there an expected outcome that is governing these things for them?

Then think of the social interactions that are permitted. Nothing inspires new activity quite like other children can. Do they have the resources and opportunities to work together on a task? Do the resources invite collaboration, perhaps by being too heavy or large to manage by themselves? You may also like to offer different social groupings as children mix with different people and a diverse mix of characters, ideas and approaches. Encourage their questions as you support them to find ways of exploring answers together.

All of this will benefit when rigid planning of your activities is avoided so that changes can naturally happen. As you become aware of and respond to expected and unexpected opportunities for learning, you can welcome diversity into your day. By being more fluid in your approach, your plans can mirror your children's interests as you respond to any opportunities, allowing the day to unfold, influenced from various sources. When flexibility can be embraced, so too can the evolving ideas and intentions that come from these moments as children learn to benefit from rather than fear new opportunities, adapting to changing situations without the feelings of stress that may otherwise accompany moments that differ from what they might expect.

Support

Be supported in offering practice, environments and experiences where this can be explored

As you look to offer children experiences intended to inspire them, begin by knowing each individual child. Only then will you find what may encourage them to become curious enough to approach different areas, to try new things and to get involved. When you know what they are interested in, you can then add new elements that are likely to appeal. Start by observing the activities you currently offer, not in terms of how well resourced you think they are, but in how well accessed and utilised they are by the children. I have seen some beautiful mud kitchens and outdoor play environments that have received substantial levels of investment, only to be completely ignored by the children. This may be because certain elements are missing, for example the usable mud and other natural "ingredients" that can be utilised. It may be because permissions or access are not well-thought through, or because other distractions or "over design" is getting in the way (Figure 12.3).

Rewarding investigations involve you arousing children's natural curiosities, together with giving them the abilities they need to follow these through. This may come from strange or unusual objects that they have little understanding of, then inviting children to investigate and consider what they are for or how they can be used. It may be from opportunities to use things they have seen adults using, having a go themselves and seeing how the experience feels for themselves. For example, using real order forms in a "café" before serving edible food, playing with real envelopes and stamps in a "post office" or performing real scientific reactions.

Figure 12.3 Look to invite your children to do new things with authentic environments that they are free to explore, with curiosity and permission to adapt.

You can encourage children to initiate the activities they do want to do and allow them opportunities to follow their ideas as closely as possible. Allow them ownership of space and open-ended resources where you can while you promote their autonomy and they experience the power of their actions. When they hit difficulties, help them to explore alternative solutions and other things they can try, adapting rather than being quick to give up.

As you show genuine interest in the things they are doing you can promote their curiosity, inspiring them to become involved in new opportunities and adapting their responses to them. Unexpected occurrences are commonplace throughout life and when we can combine this into their play, we can promote their engagement as they learn to adapt, equipping them to face any new challenge. You might want to talk to them with open-style questions that do not have just one answer. Add a related object to their play or gradually reveal resources as together you consider the next element of a story, adapting their responses accordingly.

13 Nurturing young children to be brave

Being Brave
BECOMING COURAGEOUS AND CONFIDENT

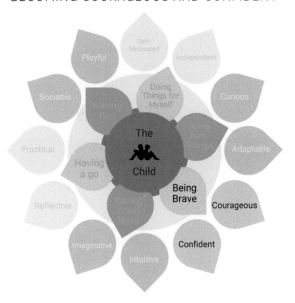

Figure 13.1 Being Brave – Becoming Courageous and Confident. When we offer a young child's opportunities to be brave, they can experience their courage and confidence in ways that permit these dispositions to develop.

In this chapter we are going to focus our attentions on nurturing young children to be brave, developing the courage and confidence to feel a greater sense of security and well-being and developing these dispositions ready to support all the experiences to come (Figure 13.1).

When we think of being brave we can often overlook the leaps of faith that our children take every day as they test their courage levels and challenge how confident

DOI: 10.4324/9781003327042-15

they feel. While our environments and the activities we plan may be well tested and commonplace to our mature levels of understanding, many of these experiences will be new to a child - and as a result, profoundly unnerving. Simply engaging with these experiences and interacting within the social groups around them will require an element of bravery while at the same time informing their beliefs in themselves as a courageous individual.

As a child joins a new environment for the first time, they are testing how confident they feel in it. Until a sense of belonging is established they will need to rely on their courage. And that will be informed by any previous positive experiences and reflected in higher levels of motivation and involvement than may otherwise be felt. Confident children are better able to make use of the potential opportunities they are being offered. They are more able to engage in new social connections, forming bonds and attachments as they settle into a new setting. And they tend to recover more quickly from setbacks as they embrace future challenges, happy to seek out the support and guidance they need to make the most of new experiences. By the time this new setting becomes the school classroom, this quickly translates into educational achievement, so it is important that we support children's feelings of bravery before they are disadvantaged from a lack of it.

Knowledge

Know why it is important for young children to be brave

As children get older, their play becomes more distanced from the adults they once relied on. Not only are they less influenced by your ideas and direction but they are now far more interested in the other children around them. However, playing with other children does in itself require an element of bravery, as children demonstrate their courage to interact and engage, along with their confidence that this will be a worthwhile endeavour.

When we consider what it means for a child to engage with a group of children who are already playing, we can see the bravery this seemingly innocent task involves. Firstly, they need to become in tune with the conversations that are already occurring; they need to understand the game, its rules and its boundaries, and then be ready with the social skills required to support the play. As the direction the play is taking is swiftly discussed and debated, challenges are considered, and the rapidly changing rules are determined.

Boys and girls do tend to show gender differences in their play and approaches to bravery at this age, with girls tending to show higher confidence levels than boys as they become more involved in these social engagements, perhaps because of their sociability and desire to conform or perhaps from the importance of the skills they tend towards, whereas boys will be more inclined to get stuck in a physical game. Either way this may demonstrate the origins of future gender differences starting to take place.

To partake in these important social exchanges, children need to find and develop their courage to have a go in the first place. They also need opportunities to voice their views as they discover the power of their voice, developing the confidence to use it. There will be many opportunities in life that will come their way and it is through these early exchanges with their peer groups that children are developing the skills that will allow them to recognise and grasp all the opportunities their futures may bring.

Understanding

Understand how to develop a young child's ability and desire to be brave

As you look to support young children, you need to establish a balanced approach. As they develop their courage and confident outlook, you must be mindful of their range of developing abilities, as well as the impact of the moment. You need to allow children to trial a range of skills for themselves, with your encouragement and guidance whilst ensur-

ing that these are accessed at the right level. Some support may be required for a child to take great leaps forward. In other circumstances, a slower, continued access to a challenge may be required for some time before a child is ready to achieve their goal. And while they may seem on the verge of a great accomplishment one day, tiredness or a coming illness may limit this tomorrow. Only through knowing the child and the moment can you allow children the positive experiences of setting themselves challenges and succeeding within them, developing the courage to persist (Figure 13.2).

Figure 13.2 Sometimes bravery comes as a giant leap of faith, other times it is tiny footsteps towards our goal. Be on hand to support but let the bravery come from them.

In this way, children find the opportunities they need to establish their own voice within social interactions. They learn what their bodies are capable of without developing a fear of trying. And they can become familiar with hitting a barrier, seeing it as a natural part of the learning process and accessing or developing the skills needed to continue. When children are given opportunities within welcoming environments to test their own boundaries, they develop the courage to push through them. Unpressured, they are not developing a fear of failure. But more than this, they are beginning to realise that not being able to do something tells them something about their skills today. It does not imply limits on their abilities tomorrow. When they then take these experiences into future learning situations, they are then ready and willing to push though the demands and challenges that academic activity will invariably bring.

However, to develop a growing confidence within a child, all their abilities must be recognised and valued. No one approach will suit the unique abilities of all children so ensure your children all have room to shine. This involves seeing and recognising a wide range of abilities, preferably within a diverse array of peer groupings and opportunities. You can do this by offering a safe environment in which they can demonstrate all their skills. This should be adaptable and secure so that they can explore possibilities, perhaps surprising themselves as well as others, mindful that to do anything less would suggest only specific skills are respected or valued.

Support

Be supported in offering practice, environments and experiences where this can be explored

As you look to support a child's developing levels of courage and confidence it is so important that you proceed at their pace, without rushing the process or expecting to meet unrealistic expectations. Once you have offered an environment in which they feel safe and secure, consider how they are feeling within it. Do they appear to engage with the items available and the other children around them with ease or does something appear to be holding them back?

Begin by looking to understand how a child is feeling about a set task or activity so that you can help develop their courage in ways that are right for them. The environment may be too noisy, too overwhelming or chaotic or may lack a degree of closeness that they are used to in other settings. It may be a reluctance to get messy or a learnt behaviour such as a fear of spiders or an unease around groups of children that is holding them back. Are they able to manage themselves and the skills that are being requested of them? Do they have opportunities to go at their own pace, offering their own ideas and alternative direction?

To support their developing confidence within the environment, offer children opportunities to engage with a diverse range of experiences and individuals. With the resources, time and permissions to try at their own pace, allow them to continue for as long as they feel comfortable, with the option to return again later if and when they feel ready. You may also like to talk to children about how they view different tasks and their role within them. As you draw attention to the efforts they are making, you can highlight the small wins that you have made possible for them.

As you look to promote their voice and opinions, ask them what they would they like to make happen? How would they like this day to go? If you have high-lighted their emotional security as some-thing that needs supporting, play games that help them find their voice and build their confidence. Support different opportunities for social interactions where they can practice social skills such as sharing, co-operation, listening and voicing ideas and allow them to take various roles within the group.

Figure 13.3 Bravery comes in all shapes and sizes, sometimes it is more about emotional separation than a physical display of confidence.

Ensure that you are encouraging and validating various skills as you celebrate each child's unique abilities through the different activities you offer. Be sure to give children unhurried and unpressured chances to try as you offer them opportunities to take control and ownership. Let them feel a sense of bravery as they explore, taking on appropriate risks and challenges. All the while be mindful of what this means to each child, allowing them to set the pace and direction (Figure 13.3).

14 Nurturing young children to have good ideas

Having Good Ideas
BECOMING INTUITIVE AND IMAGINATIVE

Figure 14.1 Having Good Ideas – Becoming Intuitive and Imaginative. When we allow a young child opportunities to have their own ideas, they experience what it means to be intuitive and to use their imagination, encouraging these dispositions to develop.

In this chapter we are going to focus our attentions on nurturing young children as they have good ideas, using their intuition and imagination to develop these powerful tools of learning (Figure 14.1).

When we give children opportunities to explore their own ideas, they begin to discover more diverse methods of thinking and doing things for themselves. When they

DOI: 10.4324/9781003327042-16

have experienced seeing these ideas realised they are more ready to challenge the abilities they have, using their imagination to push these ideas further. And once they become familiar with these techniques they are better able to see the potential of a situation and to embrace it, all of which is fuelled by their past experiences of seeing the benefits of a good idea and being able to use these ideas to inform their intuition and the logical predictions they can bring.

The ability to mentally piece together information to arrive at new solutions is also a key component of future classroom learning. When learning new concepts, a child will take previous experiences together with new information as they intuitively develop their new understanding, drawing deeper conclusions from the process as they develop the skills of knowing something about a situation without direct experience of it. Children who have had these opportunities to develop a good imagination are then ready to mentally process new challenges and so are less concerned by them, readying them for when difficulties arise within a new task, for example learning how to read an unfamiliar word. This process is being informed by all the previous examples of something similar they have experienced and is heavily influenced by the experiences they are being offered now.

Knowledge

Know why it is important for young children to have good ideas

As children begin to engage in more advanced forms of play, their imagination becomes more developed and pronounced. You will see this within the conversations and debates that occur, the elaborate plot lines that evolve and the complex games that are played. Throughout these exchanges, children are exploring their imaginations, allowing their mental abilities to develop without the constraints of reality or the limits imposed by their environment or resources. They will also be engaging in more-evolved forms of symbolic play as these roles and the items used to support them begin to follow a plan and sequential steps.

Through these experiences children are practicing what it means to process their ideas mentally without needing to see everything in real terms. Whilst this opens their world of play significantly, it is also helping with their cognitive development. As they experience thinking through what they are doing and why, they develop beyond the impulsive acts of earlier years, an essential part of more complex cognitive functions.

As children see something real come from the ideas they are having, their self-esteem can flourish. As ideas are put forward and carried out, children are motivated to practice their motor skills, social skills and language, even taking opportunities to lead the play as they identify problems and have the ideas needed to solve them. And when given opportunities to initiate their own enquiries, to try things for themselves and to make logical judgements in the moment, children get to experience their intuitive abilities. When this is given chance to develop, children become better able to predict what might come next and to know things about situations they have not yet experienced. From this comes a greater sense of security and ease, essential when experiencing new situations, environments and people. But these skills need rehearsing and exploring like any other, within safe environments and received with encouragement and recognition for their importance.

Understanding

Understand how to develop a young child's ability and desire to have good ideas

Within environments that remain adaptable and supported by adults who understand, children may lose themselves in their imaginations. As they initiate new directions and explore greater possibilities they can develop their instincts through the ideas they are permitted to see realised. They may journey to distant or made-up lands. They can assume many different roles, including those they see around them – "I will be the teacher, you can be the daddy" – and those that allow them to explore emotions and fears that would be too difficult otherwise. These may include fantasy play as the knight slays all the enemies or as firefighters or soldiers keep everyone safe.

Figure 14.2 Time, together with imagination and a few key resources are a powerful combination.

But to allow children to do these things, their time must not be overprescribed. Instead, they need to be given space and opportunity to explore their ideas, with the understanding that these are valid and exciting. You can help them to develop this mindset by embracing an imaginative approach yourself. Talk about problems without implying that there is one required solution. Invite them to use their imagination and initiate their own ideas for a way forward. As they discuss their suggestions, you can encourage children to work together, using their social and language skills in highly motivated ways. As they become more deeply engaged with the problem, offer the support, resources or opportunities to let them trial their solutions as they see their ideas being utilised (Figure 14.2).

As you let children approach investigations how they feel they should, they can experience their own intuition, unafraid of being wrong. Even when these are unlikely to work as expected, this is a tremendously powerful learning experience. Despite your more mature outlook suggesting that something is unlikely to succeed, respect the thought processes that they are going through and the learning that is going on as you let them try anyway. This can then evolve into further problem solving and adaptation opportunities as they see what occurs and the potential problems with it. You can then develop this further by talking it through afterwards.

Through their symbolic roleplay, you may like to offer children opportunities to explore current areas of difficulty. As they rehearse different roles, they can create various scenarios as they explore different ideas in their play. In this safe environment they may pretend one thing or another was said or done based on their previous experiences. You can help them to explore feelings and emotions within stories as they use their imagination to explore how things may feel to other people.

Support

Be supported in offering practice, environments and experiences where this can be explored

We can offer our children support to widen their imagination and powers of intuition through the experiences and opportunities we offer to them. This has been happening for several years now. But as they are becoming more aware of their own bodies, these opportunities can reach a new level. And with a greater knowledge of the environment and bank of past experiences to draw from they can really begin to see what they are capable of, provided these environments and the opportunities within them do not become overly prescribed or governed which will essentially overrule their imagination.

When they are using familiar play resources or following similar activities, introduce a new material or an unusual addition to support and extend their ongoing thought processes. These may offer them a different way of thinking about things or introduce a new problem that needs exploring (Figure 14.3).

Throughout the day you might like to encourage them to imagine what will come next, perhaps by considering what they know to inform their imagination. You could then follow their suggestions to see what would happen or use this opportunity to get really creative where

Figure 14.3 Introducing a different material can add a whole new dimension to their understanding.

no possibility is unreasonable. You can support these techniques further through the stories you encourage the children to make up. Offer props or cliffhangers if necessary to keep the plot line exciting and humour to promote their imaginative use of language.

As you engage with them about what they have done or if they are keen to talk about what they are doing, use these opportunities to explore their imagination. How do they think that worked? Who might this be good for? Who might come here? Avoid questions you know the answer to and instead, capture their imagination and your own, as together you engage in new thinking. I wonder what would happen if you mixed different quantities? What will it be like when it dries? What made the tower fall?

Provoke their new ideas by introducing games they need to devise rules for. As you play, consider questions that have come from how you played before. Consider solutions to any problems that may arise together as you think back through the experiences they have had before and use these experiences, along with every other interaction with children, to explore what they think about things. As you give voice to the ideas or questions they may have, you are allowing them to experience this valuable learning mechanism for themselves. You are helping them to see that nothing is a silly question or unworthy of serious thought and that all of this is within their capabilities as you further ignite a love of enquiry in your children.

15 Nurturing young children to have a go

Having a Go
BECOMING REFLECTIVE AND PRACTICAL

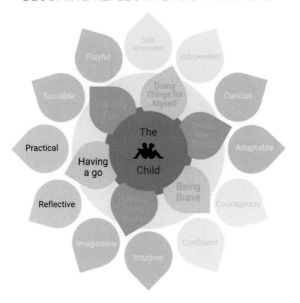

Figure 15.1 Having a Go – Becoming Reflective and Practical. When a young child is given opportunities to have a go for themselves, they can develop a wider range of practical skills and gain the experiences they need to reflect upon as these dispositions develop.

In this chapter we are going to focus our attentions on nurturing young children as they develop the abilities and desires to have a go, developing the practical skills that allow them to do so and the deeply impactful opportunities to reflect that follow (Figure 15.1).

Practical play allows children to repeatedly experience ideas in ways they can touch and see. As they do so, they are becoming familiar with theories and ideas that they will

DOI: 10.4324/9781003327042-17

later rely on in anything from a physics to a chemistry lesson. They are experiencing the techniques and core knowledge of design and technology, and they are also becoming familiar with the ways in which they can explore their knowledge through trial and improvement. While these experiences are all providing valuable techniques for future learning experiences, they are also providing the underpinning knowledge and expertise that will inform their future conceptual analysis and providing the memories and experiences children will need to later reflect on.

As every experience informs their future approaches to learning, reflective children do more than repeat experiences of the past, they learn from them, continuously improving and fine-tuning responses as they are developing their core learning skills. These experiences of tackling difficult concepts in manageable ways allow children to gain access to difficult ideas in ways they can understand. And as they learn to test and challenge what they know, they are reaffirming their understanding and exploring ways of learning that will offer the confidence to persist when these concepts are met again.

Knowledge

Know why it is important for young children to have a go

Now that children are gaining greater strength and manual dexterity they are capable of more involved "tinkering" with real tools and resources through which their ideas can really take shape as they are encouraged and inspired to try things out for themselves. When children are given these opportunities to have a go at something for themselves, they are developing scientific and technological ideas about how things work or why they did not, gained through tangible experiences that can be felt throughout their whole bodies.

This realism, when it is valued, suitably resourced and supported, allows children to explore their world, how it works and what they are capable of within it. Through the practical experiences children are offered, they gain a concrete way of experiencing some of the difficult or abstract ideas that they currently lack the knowledge to fully understand, while laying the foundations for the more advanced concepts of the future. And as they are offered free, diverse and varied explorations, children learn to identify their own problems whilst developing the skills to solve them.

Along with these practical experiences, children are gaining the memories that allow them to reflect on past experiences. When children practice moving mentally from a purely "here and now" focus they can learn to reflect on past events and consider future possibilities. These reflections allow them to think about their actions and possible alternative responses, all the while increasing their developing knowledge and understanding as they think about what occurred and learn to use these insights to consider alternative possibilities. As their imagination develops, they can then utilise these experiences in the classroom when learning about forces in physics, reactions in chemistry or the effects of rain on a plant. This supports a deeper level of understanding as children no longer need to experience every possibility to make meaning of something they are learning about.

Understanding

Understand how to develop a young child's ability and desire to have a go

When you offer children exciting or novel opportunities children will naturally want to get involved. They will be interested to see what something is all about and how they can become involved with the things you have made available (Figure 15.2). You can maximise this potential by allowing children the chance to design their own investigations, inspired by and supplied with authentic resources. You might like to get them started by suggesting a problem that needs solving or a task that needs thinking about. This could be a visitor that needs to be made welcome, real or otherwise, if you have recently shared *The tiger that came to tea*. When you supplement their play with authentic resources and issues with personal relevance, you can take their interest to a deeper level as they reflect on things they know something about.

You can also inspire greater involvement by linking an investigation or experiment to something they are personally interested in. If they have shown an interest in insects or the animals that come into the garden, you may like to invite them to design and structure different kinds of habitats. They could then reflect on how they will know whether their designs are a success or how they could entice more creatures into them. Offer them real objects and tools where you can, using these opportunities to think about risk management and respect for the things they are using and each other.

As you encourage their involvement, avoid derailing it through your own expectations or ideas. Allow them to make mistakes and to learn from them before trying again. Avoid interrupting their flow of thought and concentration by asking what they are doing or why. And wait for them to ask for help before offering it. When children do ask for help, explore the precise nature of the support they need rather than simply solving their issue for them as you help them to think about the next practical

Figure 15.2 Authentic resources, especially when they have been experienced in different environments, allow children to make deep connections within their learning.

step within their problem. In this way you are teaching valuable transferable skills, rather than reinforcing a tendency to give up.

After having experienced these opportunities together you can discuss the things that happened. What have they learnt and what they might do differently next time? How will they proceed tomorrow when they get started with the project again? You can consider the approaches that have been used, the actions of the people involved and how useful different resources may have been. You might like to make links between home, family and settings, repeating experiences so children can share what they have learnt, encouraging children to make deep connections in their learning experiences (Figure 15.3).

Support

Be supported in offering practice, environments and experiences where this can be explored

As you look to offer opportunities for your children to have a go, be mindful of their growing abilities and increasingly mature approaches. Do not be afraid to offer authentic tools and resources, with the right guidance and supervision as children experience what they can do. Know that the memories you are offering through these hands-on experiences are offering a multitude of skills that they will utilise throughout their learning journey.

Allow them time to simply "tinker" with the resources you have offered in ways that appeal to them in the moment. Permitted to naturally evolve, these moments of getting lost in possibility are far more interesting than trying to achieve a prescribed end goal, especially when you are on hand should they wish to ask questions or seek some guidance. With appropriate supervision, offer children real tools to cut wood, to slice vegetables and undo screws as they explore these techniques. Not only is this strengthening their fine- and gross-motor skills, but it is also teaching them respect for these tools and opening up their world of understanding in ways that playing with imitations can never do.

Offer children a range of resources to support their play so that practical decisions can be made along the way. Will the string or the tape be best for securing the den? Which fabric will work best?

Figure 15.3 Provide a range of materials for children to record their ideas and their progress in ways that are meaningful to them.

What happened the last time they tried? Can they manage this by themselves or do they need to engage the help of a friend? If you can also leave a challenging activity where it is for children to return to over several days, they can then consider different approaches, considering what happened and how things could be different.

Invite the children to share stories of their experiences as you reflect and learn from one another. You can use prop boxes to share their stories, adding deeper purpose and authenticity to their reflections as others are encouraged to ask questions and share ideas. These opportunities for reflection also help children develop empathy for others as they observe the tasks they have been involved in and the different reactions that have followed as together you consider how this may have felt.

Provide resources for them to record what they have learnt. This might include a range of paper and pens, but perhaps opportunities to use photography, video cameras or audio recordings too. Encourage children to revisit these as their ideas develop and they can see their progress. These also offer visual cues and reminders of past actions and consequences as you support their understanding of them. Return to them sometime later as children see the development of their practical play.

16 Nurturing young children to have fun

Having Fun
BECOMING PLAYFUL AND SOCIABLE

Figure 16.1 Having Fun – Becoming Playful and Sociable. When we offer young children opportunities to have fun, they can enjoy the playful and social experiences that having fun means, encouraging these dispositions as they develop.

In this chapter we are going to focus our attentions on nurturing young children as they have fun, developing the playful experiences and social encounters that encourage these dispositions to develop (Figure 16.1).

Play has always been and continues to be the most important method of learning for children. It offers continual opportunities for them to trial ideas without fearing

DOI: 10.4324/9781003327042-18

mistakes and to experience different processes while creating the memories that will underpin all their future learning experiences. Concepts such as weight and measure cannot be fully understood until children have experienced their effects for themselves. Challenges such as the covering of a den or the wrapping of a present offers meaningful experiences, through which children learn the importance of these concepts. The realities of peoples' lives cannot be truly considered until integral elements of them are trialled for themselves, whether this is embarking on the first voyage to the South Pole like Robert Scott or life as Blackbeard the Pirate.

When children are given opportunities to share these meaningful experiences with their friends, deeper social exchanges are prompted. As they explore distant and imagined concepts together, the need for new vocabularies grow as language ability strengthens. Children are developing their social, emotional and behavioural responses in these moments in companiable ways that avoid the behavioural difficulties that can end up restricting learning opportunities, now and in the future.

Knowledge

Know why it is important for young children to have fun

As children get older and thoughts begin to turn to more academic activities, some may be questioning the role and purpose of play. However, play remains the most powerful learning vehicle that your children will be experiencing and must not diminish, even when the start of school is approaching and preparations for it may be increasingly brought to mind.

The trouble with more traditionally academic pursuits is that focus can turn to how well a child can demonstrate their learning. While this may have a place when sitting exams in ten years' time, for your very young learner this disjointed display of conceptual ideas detracts from the intense learning that is occurring. During their engaged moments of play children are connecting their understanding of, for example, letters and numbers, to their use for them. They are laying the foundations of conceptual understanding and establishing the connections that later academic learning will rely on. It is here that their learning is happening and their need for meaningful play is as strong as ever (Figure 16.2). Focus should then remain on making these links in playful ways, avoiding any measures that seek to isolate this knowledge.

Figure 16.2 Mark making has a very real purpose in play; but it must not replace the play.

Through their play, children's understanding of concepts will be increasing and with it, more questions will be raised. Play offers a safe environment in which to explore these ideas, along with the social engagements that will further support this process. Given opportunities to play and communicate, to share ideas and learn from one another, children are discovering and strengthening their own abilities. They are developing rich vocabularies and establishing techniques for solving their own problems. Through the emotional well-being that can flourish through these exchanges, they are developing the social skills and behaviours they will rely on in the classroom, along with the confidence and voice to make the most of the learning opportunities to come.

Understanding

Understand how to develop a young child's ability and desire to have fun

As you look to the environment and its resources to engage young children in playful, sociable fun you might like to think about the opportunities you are offering them now they are older, stronger and more capable. Where you can include resources that are heavier, bulkier or more complex, you will invite collaborative engagements between children as they work together to move items or achieve their goals. Through these experiences come the natural opportunities for communication, social interaction and peer support. These will be even more engaging if you can include genuine, authentic experiences that reflect their maturing abilities.

As you continue to encourage this deeply meaningful activity with your children, be sure to validate it by ensuring the adults around them understand and promote its purpose. By knowing how they can extend play without derailing it, they may inspire further enquiry, mindful of not taking it over as they allow children's own discoveries to flourish without a preplanned agenda in mind. This also needs the time and space required for exploration, avoiding premature interruptions or breaks for routine, so, where you can, consider how you can leave their play without clearing away. When children are given opportunities to return to something that retains their interest, some projects may potentially last for weeks.

You can increase the authenticity of their play by adding genuine materials such as real food to the home corner or shop, tools in construction or items they see the adults in their lives using. Think about the actual items used at a hairdresser, a veterinary clinic or post office rather than being tempted to buy toy representations of them. If you include your local community, children's families and wider connections in your plans, this can generate some wonderful opportunities for inexpensive resourcing and coming together.

As you allow children to form their own social groupings within their play, be mindful of any children who appear to be left on the edge. You might like to include things of particular interest to them, especially if this offers them a sense of being the "expert", with frequent opportunities to meet new people or engage in different groupings through the activities you offer. If children are struggling with social interactions, observe as they engage in play, particularly where scenarios involve concepts of feelings, behaviours and emotions (Figure 16.3). As you explore subtleties of behaviour through the stories you share and the behaviours you model, you can also be a subtle presence, giving insecure children the support they need to engage.

Support

Be supported in offering practice, environments and experiences where this can be explored

As you look to promote children's meaningful play experiences, simply follow their lead. Listen to what they are interested in and supply the authentic resources and adult insight that can make these interests come alive for them. If they are interested in Antarctic exploration, you might like to talk about all the equipment they may need to be away from home. Where would they sleep? What would they eat? How would they carry everything they need and what might that feel like? As they experience this weight, build a tent for them and all their helpers to sleep in or eat some of the traditional cornbread and stew, and you can bring these ideas to life.

Offer resources for children to create their own shops, homes or adventures. By avoiding prescribing what these should look like, you can invite their imagination and voice. You might like to offer prompts or suggest some collective problem solving. "How will we build our pirate ship?" "How can we layout our shop and what should we stock it with?" Even if the shop is never customer-ready, the play involved in the preparation will be priceless.

Children will now be more interested in fantasy and risky play. This may cause some concern with families, so address this by considering why these forms of play appeal to children. Fantasy play allows them to be whomever they want, with extraordinary powers of magic or strength. For a child who may often feel powerless this is an engaging concept, and who would not want to

Figure 16.3 A common interest, such as searching for a worm can be a great way of encouraging a shy child to interact.

experience fairy wings and magic? If conflicts arise, support them to problem solve situations for themselves as they explore co-operative solutions, only intervening when needed.

Children also need to experience rough and tumble play, to manage risk and conquer their challenges. They need to get dizzy as they spin, to feel unbalanced and to feel the exhilaration of low-level fear that they can control. Find ways that these can be explored safely through their physical play and games. For example, managing the big slide, balancing on the beam or having the opportunity to take the lead in something.

If a child is struggling to engage, you can promote their social involvement by modelling some techniques with your own responses, actions and intonation with visual cues informing them of when it is time to interact. You can help connect them with experiences where they may feel more comfortable, such as offering resources from home as you help them make connections with something familiar and safe through their play. You may also like to provide resources that connect their interests with those around them, encouraging them to share what they know as they experience something they can lead on.

17 Nurturing young children to think

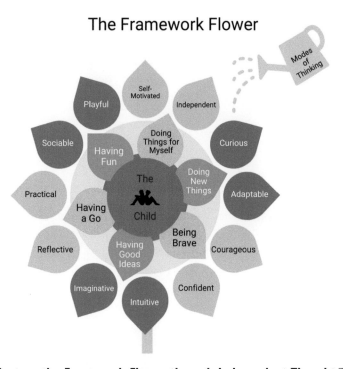

The Framework Flower

Figure 17.1 Nurture the Framework Flower through Independent Thought. Throughout all our interactions, provocations and permissions, we need to remember that we are raising independent thinkers, ready to engage and ponder, to understand and know.

As we draw this book to a close let us revisit the Framework Flower and draw our attention to the magic that allows all of this dispositional development to really take root... and that is in providing our children with the autonomy and permissions to experience what it means to think; to be creative, to simultaneously use different ideas and make connections in their leaning, to think of the bigger picture and take logical leaps (Figure 17.1).

DOI: 10.4324/9781003327042-19

As children engage in more complex learning, they are taking information in from multiple sources, all of which need evaluating at once. As they plan a journey they need to know what resources they can use, who is coming, what the weather is likely to be and how previous trips have gone. As these experiences connect areas in their thinking they are underpinning and inform the next opportunity. As creative thinkers they will be approaching these new concepts from a choice of angles, ready to embrace a range of creative solutions to new problems, provided their previous creative endeavours have been met positively and have been validated as worthwhile pursuits.

As a child's logical understanding develops they will be practicing what they know, drawn to the logic, rhythm and pattern all around them. You will see this desire emerge as they want things to follow an expected logic, possibly becoming concerned or agitated when they do not, as they look to make sense of their world. As children take their understanding beyond that which is immediately presented, they are becoming familiar with the wider nature of knowledge, recognising familiarity in new situations and concepts wherever they are encountered. All of these abilities are combining and need validating within your thinking children (Figure 17.2).

Knowledge

Know why it is important for young children to think

As a child's experiences grow, they are becoming increasingly informed by the information that is available to them. As they add to this growing bank of memories they are better able to consider new experiences, their latest challenge or the unfamiliar circumstance that is presented to them. The ability to draw on past experiences as they simultaneously bring these experiences together allows them to make better use of all the learning that has gone before. For example, as they build a den they need to know what resources they have available, who is on hand to help, where they are allowed to play and how previous techniques and methods have helped.

When given opportunities to develop their creative thinking, children can access meaning and understanding of things in unique ways. They can experiment with inventive methods and different directions that perhaps make better

Figure 17.2 Any new experience pulls on all the learning that has gone before as children simultaneously combine what they know and what they logically expect to happen next.

sense to them, and they can approach challenges with creative solutions, with the means to better manage their problems. The logical approaches they have been developing are now evolving and maturing as they begin to communicate their ideas to others. These nonverbal reasoning and logical thought processes are essential when learning to write, in understanding early number concepts and when graphic representation develops.

They will now be embracing more challenging investigations that incorporate the whole environment, with a greater need to combine their abilities and the resources and information that are available in different locations and through different means. Once in place, a child can take advantage of the powerful potential that comes from knowing what they need and where they can get it. Intuitively combining different methods of thinking and accessing information from various sources as they combine and draw new meaning is an essential set of skills going forward. It is also a key requirement of being where you are supposed to be and doing what you have been asked to do, while still being able to think while doing it.

Understanding

Understand how to develop a young child's ability and desire to think

As children utilise a varied skill set, deeper levels of thought and understanding are embraced. These different methods and approaches to thinking need to be in place for a child to manage within more complex environments. And that is before they try to understand the demands placed on them. Before thought processes and understanding reach higher levels of complexity, it is so important that we encourage different thinking skills in a child. But this requires the opportunities and permissions they need to engage in different styles of thought as they become familiar with them and what they are capable of achieving.

To develop their ability to think more widely, or to hold more than one thing in their mind at once, children need to access their memories and past experiences. For the immature mind of a child to manage this, they may need instant access to a past experience, they may need to explore it from a slightly different angle or to test something a new idea is questioning. You cannot know these thought processes in advance; your role is to have these varied experiences available within an environment that children can readily access and adapt. And as you do, allow them to combine, utilise, investigate, connect and display in ways that feel natural to them – not always how it suggests on the box.

There is also a greater need to understand and challenge the activities provided as they gather and combine information from various sources. As connections are made, children are developing a more complete understanding of a situation, drawing on their memories and the things they think they know. When you offer environments that provide creative challenges rather than more obvious results, you are stimulating this work. Encouraging children to push their intellectual boundaries as you offer them wide-reaching challenges, and to think creatively about the resources and opportunities you make available.

You can support development of their logical thought by following logical steps as together you consider how things work. You can invite them to identify connections between diverse resources that connect through different methods, giving them things to associate and talk about. They are also developing methods of expressing their abstract, hidden and imagined ideas in ways that make sense to them. So, include discussions about things they cannot see or maybe have not yet experienced. When this is done with relevant and interesting ideas of personal relevance, you can later reflect on their ideas, developing their key language within genuine and interesting topics.

Support

Be supported in offering practice, environments and experiences where this can be explored

As you look to offer children a wide variety of activities and experiences, be conscious of offering opportunities for children to think for themselves (Figure 17.3). Balance those where instruction is provided or activities initiated as you encourage choice. Offer independent explorations as well as with small groups of friends. When you do introduce activities, try to invite the child's own interpretation of them, possibly by accessing additional resources or inspiration from various sources. Then give children free access to their environment as they learn to use all the information and locations available to them.

Ensure these environments are adaptable as children create new spaces and interesting projects, using resources in creative ways, knowing they have permission to do so. You can also take this outside to limit concerns over mess, noise or disruption. With ample supplies available, invite children to work together, thinking about how to approach something or to see where their creative inspiration may take them. If you support their creative thinking by

Figure 17.3 Look to include a range of activities that require logical steps and those that children can combine for themselves, being sure to focus on the child's experience in the moment.

modelling some ideas, utilise a range of resources to demonstrate their possible uses, being careful not to restrict a child's version of the experience. And think of creativity in terms that go beyond art projects as you ask for their creative solutions to the problem of the day or their suggested activities. You can then find ways of facilitating their creative responses, with your support and direction available only when it is needed.

To develop their logical thought processes, introduce games that follow consistent steps. Talk about the logical order you do things throughout the day, perhaps making visual timelines together to help children see the natural order. You might like to demonstrate the logical steps and approaches you take to solve a problem or use a mind map as you consider these techniques together. Further encourage their interest in logical outcomes by playing with reactions, such as mixing cornflour and water, or in mechanics as you predict the path of water as it travels through gullies, observing the logical patterns that repeat each time.

You can then offer experiences that encourage their wider thinking by incorporating similarities throughout their environment. Notice repeating patterns and shapes, use familiar words in different locations or experience how a range of objects may behave in similar ways, for example balls, tubes, cars and children that can all roll down the slope. Try to provide interesting prompts to encourage them to visit less-popular locations inside and out. Perhaps a teddy bear hunt where they can search in, out, under, beside and behind. And encourage their understanding of the learning potential within all different areas available to you as you add elaborate investigations, new dimensions and interesting ideas to their wider explorations.

A final word

Whether you have worked with young children for decades or this is your first time reading about child development, I hope that this book has offered you much to think about as you look to the developing capabilities and endless possibilities of the children in your life. As it has looked to encourage your reflections on the environments and interactions you share, it has asked that you do this in ways you may not have been familiar with – considering how years of experiences are informing a child's responses today as together you make the memories that will inform the experiences they still have to come, perhaps years from now.

But of course this is not solely dependent on your influence. Your socially engaging, mobile and vocal young children will be keen to share their thoughts and opinions on pretty much anything. They will be keen to establish their presence within their environments and with influence on the activities and opportunities available, they are becoming more socially connected within friendship groups that now have greater meaning to them with significant impact on what they want to do, how they want to do it and who they want to do it with.

With so much learning to be accomplished during these early years, your children have been absorbing every potential experience for several years now, constructing their understanding of the world around them through the opportunities they have been afforded. As they have made new connections in their learning, modifying and adapting, as they have made their own meaning, they have been driven by their interests and innate desires to know and understand. Now, as these experiences are being built upon, they will be influenced by all the learning that has gone before. Have their efforts paid off? Was the process of discovery engaging and purposeful? Do they feel confident in their ability to succeed, even when this may take multiple attempts? This lifelong journey of interconnected development has then been influencing every aspect of their growth and development in infinitely unique ways since they were born. However, if

DOI: 10.4324/9781003327042-20

we then look to distil it into predetermined outcomes and desired achievements, our understanding of any child becomes diminished. Attempting to channel their interests to meet desired outcomes or valuing responses according to how they measure up against a desired criteria is then both restricting and ultimately detrimental to their identity as a capable learner.

Despite this, children can now find themselves facing an increasing focus on narrow, overly formal approaches to learning, labelled as school preparation. Childhood is a finite period of time within our lives and yet it sees staggering change with monumental effect on every facet of our lives going forward. A child's development during this time must be broad, well-rounded and holistic, where their individual, fluctuating and dynamic dispositional approaches to learning are fostered. Their right to be recognised should be valued above any locally derived construct, with opportunities to think, to question and imagine as they demonstrate their growing capabilities, to themselves as much as others. Despite this, many curriculums, programmes and approaches effectively homogenise children as they fail to acknowledge the messy constructs residing within any learning or development experience. In this model, driven by prescribed learning outcomes, it is then the child who can be found lacking or not yet "school ready", within a system that remains largely ignorant of how children learn.

Whilst some formal classroom pedagogies focusing on group learning and the accumulation of discrete skills and knowledge can be beneficial, they should be an informed and conscious decision, rather than a time-consuming mainstay of each day. If we frequently limit children's diverse approaches to social learning, informed understanding and engaged participation to time spent in large group activity we fail to acknowledge their innate behaviours. At a time when they are developing notions of themselves as a learner, this can devalue their natural learning instincts, as a child simply learns that these must somehow be wrong or maybe that they themselves are no good at learning. With clear impact on their future education, this also has knock on effects within every aspect of their personal, professional and academic lives, affecting their physical health, their social-emotional well-being and ultimate life trajectories. As influential adults in a child's life, we do then have the duty and privilege to nurture their ongoing love of learning in all its forms, recognising that there is so much more to a developing child than their set of achieved milestones.

Dynamic developmental features are also embedding as children's individual, fluctuating and holistic approaches to learning are being experienced – which we can capture and nurture as we learn to recognise their responses within a wide range of environments, opportunities and social groupings, as children demonstrate their ideas, their intuition and confident approaches to new opportunities. We do then need pedagogies that are mindful of how a child engages, that are capable of capturing their interconnected developments and illustrate the practices that encourage children to become more advanced in their thinking as they become better able to demonstrate their ideas. Only then can we understand the effects we are having as we nurture development of the skills our children will need to function within a society of tomorrow that we cannot begin to imagine today.

Twenty years from now, our children will inhabit a world that we cannot possibly predict. To prepare them for this, there are then more useful skills than displays of knowledge that are increasingly available at our fingertips. Our children need to experience managing new problems within unexpected situations and evolving environments. They need to grapple with and pursue complex ideas, observing how their ideas and continued efforts can result in success. They need to be comfortable exploring alternative directions with courage and insight, together with the ability to offer opinions, to contribute ideas and work collaboratively. And as they encounter setbacks, to do so with a growth mindset, informed by previous experiences of applying the motivation and perseverance they need to succeed, unconstrained by the pursuit of one desired answer.

Through approaches that consciously remove attention from learning outcomes or the development goals being measured elsewhere, the Nurturing Childhoods Pedagogical Framework (NCPF) and the techniques shared throughout this series of books offers a profound exploration of the growth and development of children. But it does so by encouraging this shift in perspective as we look beyond the "what should we be doing?" of development guidelines and learning objectives, to look at "why should we be doing it?" – empowering you as you facilitate the opportunities that nurture your children, mindful of their depth of engagement, their behaviours and reasoning strategies and the outcomes being realised, both in the moment and as their predispositions take root.

But to embrace this new way of valuing a child's achievements, we need to take the time and space to pause for a moment, to ask ourselves about our intentions and look beyond "because this is what is expected". We need to think about our actions and what informs them, the gifts we want to send our children into the future with and the capabilities that will allow them to thrive. We need to think about how we continue to ignite their love of learning and discovery as they explore more complex ideas in increasingly independent ways. As their cognitive abilities develop, we need to look at more advanced opportunities for learning and applying their knowledge, and as their social and emotional development matures, consider how they can learn from one another, express themselves through every interaction, stimulation and permitted experience.

The pedagogical recommendations offered throughout this series are then focused on nurturing these lifelong processes of intellectual curiosity and learning as children continue on their lifelong journey of interconnected development. They look to support the adults around them to actively consider the opportunities being offered and the impact that key experiences are having on a child's developing propensity towards dispositional engagement. As children become more experienced within their environment, engagements and social interactions, it presents techniques that offer insight into how these are developing.

By focusing attention on children's dispositional development, the NCPF captures a comprehensive and holistic understanding of children's experiences of learning and development, shaped through social and environmental influences and governed through the permissions and limitations surrounding them. In doing so, these books then challenge us to view child development in practice as a deep-rooted, continuous process influenced by the child, their environment and the nurturing being provided. They look at the autonomy a child needs to explore their world and express themselves, both verbally and physically, and the experiences that allow children to make decisions, take risks and develop their sense of belonging – seen, heard and valued for all that they are. These books are mindful of themes such as communication, language and play, as well as the importance of emotional understanding and socially supportive environments that are woven throughout the series.

Through early years discourse, training and ongoing professional development, the Nurturing Childhoods approach can be used by practitioners, leaders, policy makers and anyone interested in the underpinning significance and potential we have on the life-trajectories of our children. Through parenting courses, groups and online communities, families can learn to nurture their whole child, harnessing their natural instincts for learning. As we learn to see and nurture the full potential of children by understanding, embracing and facilitating their intrinsic methods of development, while realising that none of this is possible if we don't first recognise the importance of well-being and its inseparable relationship with a child's environment, engagements and permissions – in doing so, we recognise the profound impact we have on a child's life-long journey through every decision we make.

By demonstrating the impact of experience on children's responses, their motivations and their ability to engage, these books also illustrate why so many children can present as disengaged and disconnected from their learning, a devastating observation when this is after all the most basic of natural human instincts. Surrounding children with adults who understand the intricacies of development is then paramount as we think about the messages we send through the experiences we offer. How do we convey our expectations, our limitations and our empowerments throughout the environment? How do we encourage children to explore and what are our reactions when they do? How do we respond to their ideas when they are very different to what we may have been expecting? We do then need to look through more than our adult agendas. We need to imagine what it means to be the child in front of you. What are their motivations? What responses do they feel compelled to demonstrate, and where do they have a choice, a voice and a degree of autonomy? We also need to inspire this level of understanding in all the influential gatekeepers, determining the nature of our children's experiences.

Throughout this series, I hope to support you as you look beyond any curriculums, guidelines or qualifications, guiding you to see the whole child. Through the knowledge, understanding and frameworks presented, I want to inspire you to reflect on your environments, interactions and the experiences you share, and through their truest form of communication, know how your children are responding to your provocations, as you notice their behaviours and the underpinning dispositions they reveal. When we can place children at the heart of our thinking and remain aware of their evolving dispositions, we can gain a clear picture of who they are, both in the moment and as you inform every future experience they have to come. When we begin to see the holistic nature of their experiences, we can have a far greater appreciation for the impact we are having as gatekeepers to these experiences. We can recognise how well we entice deep-rooted characteristics through our provocations and how the messages our children receive, both intentionally and otherwise, are informing their sense of self, both in the moment and as experiences that will inform every experience to come.

In the first book in this series we looked at the needs and developments of pre-verbal children not yet able to freely navigate the world around them. We then moved our attentions to toddlers getting to their feet and exploring more independently as they develop the powerful tools of learning they were born with. In this book we have focused on children with a few more years' worth of experiences influencing all they do. In the fourth book of the series we will then explore the different realities faced by children as they enter more formal environments of learning. We will look at further tools and methods used to capture classroom pedagogies and their impact, empowering you with techniques to observe, reflect on and nurture your children's innate abilities and inclinations to thrive.

There is also a setting-based Accreditation and a suite of online courses for parents, practitioners and teachers for you to explore at the Nurturing Childhoods Academy and the Nurturing Childhoods Community, where you can share your experiences and receive tons of support and guidance, so for more information head to academy. nurturingchildhoods.co.uk.

Index

Pages in *italics* refer to figures and pages followed by "n" refer to notes.